Get Out of Your Head and Into Your Body

A SOMATIC THERAPY GUIDE TO OVERCOME PTSD, TRAUMA, AND STRESS

ALEXANDRA OLSEN

TABLE OF CONTENTS

YOUR FREE GIFT

Inside the book, you will discover:

- The right way to breathe while meditating
- What position works best for you
- How to practice Mindfulness, Loving-Kindness, and Body Scan Meditation
- And much more

To get the free Gift, go to

bit.ly/free_bonus_content

INTRODUCTION

Healing is never a universal journey. On the topic of healing alone, there are a million approaches, two million books, and millions more people struggling to understand which doorway labeled "healing" is the right one for them. Approximately six of every hundred people in America alone suffer from post-traumatic stress disorder (PTSD) or some other form of trauma, which is a staggering statistic for just one of hundreds of countries worldwide (How Common is PTSD in Adults, n.d.).

Sometimes, it can feel like the process of treating trauma is harder than the trauma itself. Your trauma is, for all intents and purposes, complete; however, the memories, physical aftershocks, and coping that follow are like a never-ending whirlpool of struggle, and treatment is just one more facet that shows how much harder living with PTSD can be. You feel as though nothing is going to help, or maybe everything can help but you don't know where to start. It's overwhelming and confusing; I know that as well as anyone.

One of the paths that you can take to healing is somatic therapy. While it's an approach that may not be the first choice for everyone, something led you here today—the title of the book, a calling to dive into the world of healing, or maybe even a gut feeling that this is where you should be right now. Whatever brought you here today, you're in the right place. This book is going to take you through a journey of somatic therapy for enhanced recovery and symptom management.

Somatic therapy is unlike any other form of therapy you've already tried. This body-centered therapeutic method is an innovative yet effective approach to treating PTSD. It involves modifying how your mind and body respond to trauma-related stress, ultimately helping you harness peace and recovery within your life. Inside this guide to the world of somatic therapy, just a portion of what you will uncover includes:

- Deep insight into just what somatic therapy is and how the mind-body connection comes into play, empowering you to understand this journey from ground zero.
- The science of trauma in the body, including how trauma is impacting you—even in ways you don't notice immediately.
- How to prepare for somatic therapy, followed by a three-part guide for self-directed somatic therapy work.
- Everything you need to combine somatic therapy with other treatment modalities for a holistic approach to healing and success.

And that's just the start.

With this book by your side, you couldn't be in a better place to look at your PTSD and trauma recovery from a new lens—one that offers fresh perspectives and true results when it comes to healing. By the end of this book, you will feel refreshed. While I can't guarantee perfect healing from PTSD, I can guarantee that you will be more confident in your ability to find peace through embracing somatic therapy.

So what are you waiting for? Let's dive into this intricate journey and help you recover your true self—a version of you uncompromised by the daily effects of PTSD.

CHAPTER 1: UNDERSTANDING SOMATIC THERAPY

Healing may not be so much about getting better, as about letting go of everything that isn't you – all of the expectations, all of the beliefs – and becoming who you are.

—Rachel Naomi Remen

Somatic therapy is a concept that not many people are familiar with, yet it stands apart as a marvel of recovery and healing. There are thousands of forms of therapy, and several are tailored specifically to aiding in PTSD and trauma recovery. Why choose somatic therapy among other methods? What even is somatic therapy in the first place?

Somatic therapy is the most effective bridge between the mind and body. It connects the physical and mental areas of human experience. That might not make sense to you now, but over the course of this chapter, you'll uncover the core principles of somatic therapy and what makes it such a magnificent form of healing. Understanding the basic concepts of somatic therapy will allow you to get the most out of this holistic therapeutic modality.

The Basics of Somatic Therapy

What is somatic therapy? It's not like traditional therapeutic methods. Somatic therapy isn't going to land you on a high-dollar therapist's couch talking about how something makes you feel. While this method can be effective, it's not the most effective or the sole method for many people on the road to recovery.

Somatic therapy acknowledges the fact that the mind is valuable but highlights the fact that the body serves as an infallible repository of knowledge. In other words, our body keeps track of our trauma and the influences of it in a way that the brain may not be able to. Somatic therapy acknowledges that physical experiences, sensations, movements, and more aren't just something to be considered from the sidelines; they are central to our well-being—physically, emotionally, and psychologically. Simply put, somatic therapy considers the fact that our bodies are crucial to healing even the most psychologically rooted issues.

Core Concepts

Somatic therapy relies upon a few different concepts—ones that outline how we understand and interact with our bodies through trauma recovery and somatic therapy in particular. Understanding those core concepts will not only empower you to understand somatic therapy in depth, but also allow you to apply the concepts of somatic therapy to your own life.

The first concept to understand within the context of somatic therapy is bodily awareness. Body awareness rests at the core of somatic therapy. You have to be aware of your body and the sensations that it is experiencing in order to parse through trauma and attain recovery. Those who frequently work with somatic therapy as a main point of healing notice the subtle nuances involved in their bodily sensations.

As a result of bodily awareness, one can hone awareness of their emotional landscape. For example, many therapists recommend paying attention to the outward indicators of your emotions—like a rapid pace of heart associated with panic. By remaining tuned into the physical sensations of your body, you garner the ability to decipher the intricate language that your body speaks with regard to your trauma, emotions, and needs.

Somatic therapy also emphasizes the concept of breath and movement. How we breath, move, and otherwise engage in simple motions is vital for us to consider when thinking about somatic therapy. One example of how movement and the body intertwine for healing is through therapeutic massages. During these sessions, a massage therapist works to free "trapped" trauma from different parts of the body that hold it.

Similarly, somatic therapy often employs sessions of breathing and regulated movement to free trauma from the body and induce recovery. Breath and movement can unlock emotional reservoirs. Within somatic therapy, breath is thought of as a vehicle for regulating your emotional states; movement is the catalyst for emotional release and integration.

In other words, breath is the key and movement is the lock, each part contributing to a chain reaction of release and opening up.

Then there is the aspect of mindfulness and presence that is ingrained in somatic therapy. When it comes to somatic therapy, being aware of the present moment is crucial. Mindfulness in correlation with somatic therapy encourages you to be fully present with your experiences, which fosters a profound connection with yourself and the present moment. This becomes a highlight of how you can explore and process your emotions with a mentality of clarity and acceptance.

Other concepts certainly play a role in somatic therapy, but the body and its movements, as well as the present moment, are of the utmost importance. It might seem impossibly challenging to form a connection with these aspects of yourself, but don't worry; this book will provide step-by-step guidance for appreciating your body, movement, presence, and much more.

The Mind-Body Connection in Healing

Why does somatic therapy work, and why is the body so important when it comes to facing trauma and recovery? Trauma is something that exists, in a sense, in the mind. You experience trauma psychologically, and that impacts you on an intricate basis. Because of the mind-body connection, what your mind experiences, your body also experiences. Understanding the mind-body connection when it comes to healing and somatic therapy gets you one step closer to healing and recovery.

Somatic therapy relies heavily on the idea of a mind-body connection, which is due to the fact that somatic therapy heavily explores the connection between the mind and body in order to promote holistic healing that focuses on all aspects of the human experience. In fact, the term "somatic" is derived from the Greek word *soma,* meaning "living body." This highlights somatic therapy's deeply rooted connection with the mind-body symbiotic relationship.

Somatic therapy also strives to recognize that emotional and psychological issues aren't just rooted in the mind; they're also anchored into the body through movement, sensation, and more. This is easily viewed through certain scents and textures, and even physical movements can bring back traumatic memories for many individuals who have PTSD. If PTSD were solely a mental concept, then the physical body wouldn't play such a foundational role in the experience of the disorder.

When it comes to understanding the mind-body connection in somatic healing, there are six main principles that you will need to understand. Each principle contributes something unique and powerful to the realm of somatic therapy, so let's talk about those principles now!

Embodied Experience

The first of the six principles involved in the mind-body connection is the principle of embodied experience. The principle of embodied experience revolves around somatic therapy's focus on the here and now. In other words, it focuses on the present moment and your embodiment—or physical presence—in that moment. This is an important concept because those who practice somatic therapy believe that the body holds memories, trauma, experiences, and more—even ones that the brain does not. By tapping into the body and the present moment, therapeutic guidance can lead to the exploration of emotional and psychological states pertaining to the body and past trauma.

Body Awareness

Next, we have body awareness, which is different than embodied experience. Embodied experience focuses on the present moment and being a fully active participant inside of that moment. On the other hand, body awareness calls attention to heightened awareness of bodily sensations. This includes sensations like tension, temperature, movement, or even relaxation. During a somatic therapy session, a professional would typically guide you through tuning into these sensations, empowering you with the ability to understand your emotions and express them. In turn, this improves self-awareness and emotional regulation-related skills.

Breath Movement

Another principle of the somatic therapy mind-body connection is breath movement. Within somatic therapy, the mind-body connection is further explored by the culmination of breathing patterns and how they align with movement to help us release our physical and emotional tensions. This is important to the process of somatic therapy, as it allows you to connect with your body, release any emotions that are stored, and otherwise promote an enhanced sense of well-being.

Mindfulness

Somatic therapy also emphasizes the concept of mindfulness in the mind-body connection. When you engage with mindfulness, you gain the ability to interact with your thoughts and emotions from a space of non-judgment. This includes any emotions, sensations, or stored trauma that may be linked to your body more than your mind. Through mindfulness, somatic therapy allows you to observe without labeling, thus working to heal wounds in the body and the mind.

A Neurobiological Approach

The mind-body connection in somatic therapy also hinges on the fact that somatic therapy makes use of a neurobiological approach. This entails specific examinations of how trauma impacts the nervous system—yet another way that the body can be the holder of trauma. Because of the mind-body connection through the nervous system, somatic therapists will often work with patients to empower the regulation of the autonomic nervous system. Such work, including grounding and body-centered therapy, can help alleviate stress and anxiety surrounding trauma.

Expressive Techniques

It can be much harder to explore emotions and thoughts that are stored in the body rather than the mind. Therefore, somatic therapy often encourages the use of expressive techniques like art, movement, and other forms of nonverbal communication to bypass cognitive defenses and tap into deeper emotional experiences.

The ultimate goal of somatic therapy is the integration of body and mind. By addressing physical sensations and movements alongside emotional and cognitive aspects, you can achieve a more comprehensive and sustainable form of healing than with other modes of therapy that don't consider the mind-body connection.

Somatic therapy relies heavily on the mind-body connection, which might seem standard now that you know what the mind-body approach is and what is can do for trauma recovery; however, many forms of psychotherapy and talk therapy neglect to recognize that the body can hold trauma—despite the countless studies that prove it does. That said, your newfound understanding of mind-body principles for somatic therapy will be foundational to your healing.

Somatic Therapy: Main Principles

The previous principles explored the mind-body connection in detail, but that's not all that matters within the context of somatic therapy! Now we have to explore the main principles of somatic therapy together as an overarching concept.

For example, somatic therapy as a whole takes a more holistic perspective to healing. Where other methods might only consider the mind, somatic therapy takes a look at not just the mind and body, but also your emotions and your soul or spiritual being, in a sense. This means that your recovery will not just be isolated to one area of life; instead, the benefits that you sustain will extend into every part of your life. Practitioners achieve this holistic effect by recognizing the interconnected nature of our lives to address patients as people, not their individual symptoms.

In addition, I mentioned the mind-body connection earlier. The mind-body connection itself is a principle of somatic therapy as a whole. Somatic therapy recognizes that our emotions and experiences are stored in the body and how it feels and moves. This extends to somatic theory practices by making use of bodily movements and experiences in order to gain insight into our emotional and psychological states. Attention is given to how thoughts and emotions are expressed and held in the body.

Embodiment and awareness are key principles involved with somatic therapy. This involves being aware of your present moment bodily sensations, empowering you to engage with self-discovery and healing. As discussed earlier, a somatic therapist would encourage you to focus on different bodily sensations like heat and tension, thus allowing you to understand your current emotional experiences in a deeper capacity.

Furthermore, somatic therapy encourages mindfulness and presence so that you can observe the present moment without judgment. This means that you can reduce the reactivity you have to an experience, making it easier to parse through the way that you feel and learn to manage your symptoms. Being present helps you feel confident in understanding your emotions while overcoming traumatic experiences.

The regulation of the nervous system is also key to a successful somatic therapy experience. Your nervous system is responsible for how you respond to stress and trauma, which means that regulating it can help you avoid panic, anxiety, and other harrowing symptoms of PTSD. This is done with specific techniques aimed toward helping patients move from states of hyperarousal or hypoarousal to a more balanced and regulated state of mind.

Perhaps most fundamentally, somatic therapy works from a framework of individual-centered empowerment. It's not like traditional therapeutic methods where you are guided by the therapist; rather, somatic therapy involves collaborative efforts to achieve the results you seek, resulting in more confidence and control on the part of the individual. And because this book focuses on helping you guide yourself through the process of somatic therapy, empowerment is bound to occur.

With that being said, you now have a fundamental understanding of somatic therapy and its principles. In order to make strides toward recovery, however, you also need to understand how trauma works in the body and why the body often hangs onto traumatic experiences, sometimes harder than our minds do! That's what we're going to focus on in Chapter 2.

CHAPTER 2: THE SCIENCE OF TRAUMA IN THE BODY

Trauma victims cannot recover until they become familiar with and befriend the sensations in their bodies. Being frightened means that you live in a body that is always on guard. Angry people live in angry bodies.

—Bessel A. van der Kolk, *The Body Keeps the Score: Brain, Mind, and Body in the Healing of Trauma*

It is a common misconception that trauma is a uniquely psychological experience. Not only does the book *The Body Keeps the Score: Brain, Mind, and Body in the Healing of Trauma* serve as a foundational examination of trauma and the body, but many other bodies of scientific literature back its findings. Ultimately, these works support the idea that the body hangs on to our trauma, which influences how we let go of and process trauma.

In this chapter, we take a look at the science of trauma in the body, including what we know about why the body hangs on to trauma even when the mind does not. By the end of this chapter, you will have completed your foundational knowledge of somatic therapy. Therefore, you will be ready to delve into preparing for the self-guided somatic therapy experience.

How Trauma Impacts the Body

Trauma isn't just stored within the body; it also impacts the body. Countless people experience pain, sickness, and other symptoms that all stem from unresolved trauma due to the profound impact of trauma on the body. Understanding the main impacts of trauma on the body serves to enlighten your personal understanding as well as set the framework for comprehending how the body can keep the score of traumas.

Hyperarousal

Hyperarousal is one of the primary symptoms associated with PTSD and other trauma-related ailments. Hyperarousal involves a heightened state of psychological and physical awareness, often making those who experience it feel alert or on edge. As a result, you may notice that you are more vigilant, easier to startle, and cannot seem to "chill out." What's more is that hyperarousal can manifest as a bodily state in many ways:

- **Increased heart rate and blood pressure**: You may have heard of the "fight or flight" response. During this state, the body responds naturally to a perceived threat and thus elevates the heart rate and blood pressure. This is done to respond rapidly to danger, but it's quite troubling when you don't have a reason to feel this state of hyperarousal (since the traumatic event is over).

- **Muscle tension and pain**: Hyperarousal can make your muscles feel tense and therefore lead to pain. Because the body cannot lapse out of its heightened awareness, your muscles may contract and remain tense. As a result, you might suffer from headaches, back pain, and overall physical discomfort.
- **Hypervigilance**: Naturally, a state of hyperarousal leads to one of hypervigilance. This means that you will feel like you're on high alert and on a constant lookout for any threats. It can be an exhausting state mentally and physically, resulting in overwhelming tiredness and sleep issues.
- **Sleep disturbance**: Hyperarousal also leads to sleep disturbances. After all, you cannot sleep very well if you're constantly on edge and think the world around you is a threat. This can promote insomnia, a feeling of being unable to stay asleep, and lower quality sleep.
- **Stomach issues**: Many people who deal with hyperarousal symptoms also report gastrointestinal or stomach problems as a main symptom. This is because the chronic stress of constant hypervigilance impacts the digestive system. The gut-brain connection is what allows this to occur in the first place.
- **Memory and concentration impairment**: Being trapped in a persistent state of hyperarousal can result in memory and concentration-related impairment, leading to challenges for individuals who try to

concentrate, recall, or otherwise interact with memory.

- **Emotional dysregulation**: Someone who manages constant hypervigilance and hyperarousal may also struggle with emotional dysregulation, leading to anger, mood swings, and irritability.
- **Increased cortisol**: Cortisol is one of the body's stress hormones. When you face a stressful incident, your cortisol levels rise—which then impacts other areas of your mental and physical health.
- **Compromised immunity**: Prolonged stress can also weaken the immune system, making you more susceptible to illness and infection.

The severity and frequency of hyperarousal may vary, but if you experience it, then you likely deal with the aforementioned physical consequences as well.

Physical Illness From Trauma and Anxiety

In addition to the hyperarousal symptoms and impacts, trauma and the anxiety that stems from it can actually cause major changes to your health. Particularly, long-term trauma and relative anxiety can result in physical illness. Outside of the aforementioned hyperarousal impacts, some of the influences of trauma and anxiety on physical illness include the following:

- **Cardiovascular issues**: The chronic stress and anxiety suffered as a result of PTSD, trauma, or general anxiety can result in the development of cardiovascular/heart-related troubles. For example, it can elevate your blood pressure, heart rate, and risk of heart disease.

- **Gastrointestinal disorders**: There are a significant number of people with PTSD who also have irritable bowel syndrome (IBS) or another stomach-related disorder. This is because prolonged stress can lead to issues with the digestive system due to the gut-brain connection.
- **Immune suppression**: Under copious amounts of stress, the body can begin to suppress its own immune system. This means that it will be easier for you to get sick, and if you do get sick, it will be far harder for you to recover—even if it's just the common cold.
- **Respiratory ailments**: Anxiety and panic frequently come along with hyperventilation, which can exacerbate the symptoms of respiratory conditions like asthma. Prolonged exposure to stress can also cause the development of a respiratory disorder.
- **Sleep disorders**: Trauma and anxiety are often linked with sleep disorders like insomnia and sleep apnea. When you develop a sleep disorder, not only does it become harder to function in day-to-day life, but it also becomes harder to navigate trauma and emotions.
- **Hormone imbalance**: Chronic stress from trauma and anxiety also has the power to influence natural hormone balances. For women especially, this can

mean irregular menstruation, damaged reproductive health, or even hormonal disorders.

- **Weight fluctuations and disordered eating**: Those who face chronic stress, anxiety, or trauma often have a tenuous relationship with food. They may overeat or undereat or develop eating disorders like anorexia nervosa or binge eating disorder (BED).
- **Skin conditions**: Emotional stress can prompt flare ups of skin conditions like eczema, acne, and psoriasis, leading to a stark decline in skin health.
- **Compromised reproductive health**: Due to the hormonal fluctuations and heightened levels of stress in and of themselves, reproductive abilities may be restricted. This can mean disruptions with conceiving or maintaining a healthy pregnancy.

This explains why a lot of people head to the doctor, only to be told that their illness has no source. The source is trauma, which doesn't show up on any blood work test.

Chronic Pain

Chronic pain is another major ailment that comes alongside trauma and stress. Chronic pain refers to pain that exists for a prolonged period of time, either extending beyond a normal healing time for a particular condition or becoming recurring without relief. The link between chronic pain and trauma is complex and multifaceted, especially due to the fact that trauma can cause chronic pain—and not just physical trauma.

When one experiences something traumatic, it prompts alterations in their body on a physiological level. For example, the nervous system may become more sensitive to outside stimuli, and the body may produce more stress hormones in response. As a result, the nervous system will react differently, potentially making your brain more sensitive to pain signals. These changes can also contribute to the onset of chronic pain, as the brain isn't quite sure how to process traumatic data.

In addition, trauma can lead to something called central sensitization. This is a specific term referring to the increased sensitivity of the nervous system in response to trauma, thus resulting in a heightened perception of pain signals. Due to this, something that isn't painful might seem painful, and something that is only slightly painful can feel like being hit by a bus. In other words, trauma can potentially strip your body and nervous system of the ability to perceive pain (and other sensations) in a normal way.

There is also research revolving around emotional pain and the fact that, in some people, it may manifest physically! When you endure trauma, you also endure emotional pain. That pain is something you can end up carrying with you even after the traumatic event is over, and that actually impacts your potential development of chronic pain. For those with central sensitization, PTSD, or other disorders, that emotional pain can manifest as physical pain through the mind-body connection.

Furthermore, stress itself can cause significant amounts of bodily pain for someone with trauma. This is because stress makes the body think that something is wrong. In response, to fight off that "something," the body may produce inflammation and tension. But since some heat will not fend off trauma, all you feel is pain. Moreover, the increases in stress hormones like cortisol can lead to the development of a chronic pain condition.

There is also always the possibility of feeling pain due to the fact that trauma can give rise to psychosomatic symptoms. Much like emotional pain can manifest as physical, your psychological symptoms from trauma—including anxiousness, paranoia, and so on—can turn into psychosomatic manifestations of pain. For many people, medical care is of no use because professionals who don't consider trauma cannot source a clear cause for the pain.

Additionally, trauma can make it hard to cope with pain in the first place. Many people who suffer from trauma develop maladaptive coping mechanisms, such as substance abuse, to handle their emotional pain. Such substances and other poor choices in coping mechanisms can make it even harder for the body to fend off pain, which also contributes to the development of pain-related disorders.

Finally, chronic pain can serve as a somatic expression of unresolved emotional conflict. In other words, you might develop chronic pain due to the brain saying, "Hey, we still have something to resolve!" This can also lead to reexperiencing your trauma through the lens of chronic pain as the mind and body fight to come to a solution.

That said, chronic pain isn't a desirable symptom. Anyone who has it will tell you that it makes life a true nightmare. For those who suffer from interlocking PTSD and chronic pain, learning to manage chronic pain and traumatic symptoms through healthy outlets—including self-guided somatic therapy—can be life-changing.

The varied impacts of trauma on the body contribute significantly to why so many trauma survivors struggle to feel comfortable and safe in their own body—including the inability to have any sense of well-being. But *why,* exactly, does trauma influence the body in such an intense manner?

The Role of the Nervous System in Trauma and Healing

It all comes back to the nervous system. The nervous system isn't a body part, it is a mechanism of the body through which our experiences, perceptions, and more are filtered. It's time to gain an understanding of the nervous system and its role in trauma and healing so that we can truly jumpstart this process.

Understanding the Nervous System

In order to understand how trauma impacts the nervous system, you have to first understand what the nervous system is and does. The nervous system is broken into two subsidiary systems, the central and peripheral nervous systems, and each one plays a distinct role in your body and how you engage with trauma.

The central nervous system is made up of the brain and the spinal cord. This is the command center for the rest of the nervous system, acting as the manager. Within this central nervous system duo, the brain is responsible for processing information, making decisions, and coordinating various bodily functions, while the spinal cord, an extension of the brain, facilitates communication between the brain and the peripheral nervous system.

Then, we have the peripheral nervous system (PNS). This is made up of the nerves and the ganglia—a cluster of nerve cell bodies. Both reside outside of the brain and spinal cord. The peripheral nervous system itself is divided into two components:

1. **Somatic nervous system**: This part of the PNS is associated with voluntary movements and sensory information. It controls skeletal muscles and facilitates the conscious perception of sensory stimuli, allowing individuals to interact with their environment.
2. **Autonomic nervous system**: The autonomic nervous system regulates involuntary bodily functions, including heart rate, digestion, respiratory rate, and glandular activity. The ANS is further divided into the sympathetic and parasympathetic nervous systems:
    a. **Sympathetic nervous system**: Often referred to as the "fight or flight" system, the sympathetic nervous system prepares the body for action in response to stress or

danger. It increases heart rate, dilates pupils, and redirects blood flow to muscles, preparing the body for a rapid response.

b. **Parasympathetic nervous system**: Known as the "rest and digest" system, the parasympathetic nervous system promotes relaxation and recovery. It slows heart rate, constricts pupils, and facilitates processes like digestion and nutrient absorption.

That's quite a lot to take in, but understanding how each role of the nervous system pieces together like a puzzle can help you navigate the impact of trauma on the functions of the entire nervous system. And speaking of functions, we do have to discuss some of the main functions:

- **Sensory input**: When you receive sensory input—like when you touch something, feel pain or temperature, see something, and so forth—your nervous system receives this input. It's also responsible, in part, for decoding and interpreting that information.
- **Integration**: Once sensory input is received, the central nervous system is responsible for integrating that information. This means that the central nervous system strives to make sense of what it has received, letting the brain parse through the data. When the nervous system sustains trauma, this process is interrupted.

- **Motor output**: Based on the information received through integration, the nervous system sends motor commands to muscles and glands, directing voluntary and involuntary responses. This motor output allows for movements, actions, and physiological adjustments. In cases of trauma, motor responses may be disproportionate to reality.
- **Homeostasis**: In addition, the nervous system plays a crucial role in maintaining internal balance or homeostasis. It regulates vital functions such as body temperature, blood pressure, and glucose levels to ensure optimal conditions for cellular function.
- **Communication**: The nervous system is also responsible for various aspects of bodily communication. The nerve cells of your body, also known as neurons, transmit electrical impulses and chemical signals to convey information rapidly and precisely. They serve as chemical messengers for your whole body.
- **Adaptation**: The nervous system enables the body to adapt to changes in the environment. This can involve immediate responses to external stimuli or longer-term adaptations, such as learning and memory.

With this in mind, it's probably clear how trauma can impact the nervous system—and how such a major impact on the nervous system can create trouble for your whole body, your mind, and your spirit.

The Nervous System and Trauma

The impact that trauma can have on the nervous system is profound. It can influence the structure and function of the nervous system in a way that impacts physical, emotional, and psychological functioning and sensations. Furthermore, traumatic experiences dysregulate the body's stress response systems and alter the functioning of the central and peripheral nervous systems.

One way that trauma impacts the nervous system is by activating the sympathetic nervous system. This is what's responsible for the characteristic fight or flight response that many people associate with PTSD. Because of the activation of your sympathetic nervous system, you enter into a heightened state of arousal that allows you to react to perceived threats, as mentioned when we discussed hyperarousal.

In addition, because of the way trauma impacts your nervous system, you may have an increased startle response. This means that you react more harshly to being startled or are easier to startle. Paired with an astute sense of hypervigilance, it can feel like the entire world is frightening. Then, because your body cannot regulate its responses to fear—such as an increased heart rate—it becomes challenging to calm down.

Trauma also results in the sensitization of the amygdala. The amygdala is the part of the brain that is responsible for processing fear and emotions, which makes sense when you consider the impact of trauma on this part of the brain.

In other words, trauma influences the way your brain processes emotion and fear—and not in a good way. This heightened sensitivity may lead to an increased emotional response to stimuli associated with the traumatic experience or stimuli that is similar in any way.

Furthermore, trauma and its influence on the nervous system can result in hypothalamic-pituitary-adrenal (HPA) axis dysregulation. The HPA axis, a key component of the body's stress response system, may become dysregulated in response to trauma. This can result in altered cortisol levels, impacting the body's ability to regulate stress and modulate the immune response.

Changes in brain structure can also accompany trauma. Some people feel symptoms pertaining to dissociation or emotional numbing as a coping mechanism in response to trauma, which can lower your ability to connect with emotions, sensations, or awareness. This, then, affects how experiences are integrated by the nervous system.

It might sound rather disparaging to hear all of the ways that trauma impacts your nervous system and therefore you as a whole person, but it is through this understanding that you gain the ability to heal and recover. Now we take a look at how knowledge of the nervous system can be used in conjunction with PTSD and trauma healing.

The Nervous System and Healing

The nervous system has a grip on healing in various ways, including but not limited to the following:

- In PTSD, your stress response symptom becomes unregulated, resulting in heightened arousal, hyperreactivity to stressors, and difficulties in returning to a baseline state of relaxation. Healing can balance these symptoms and benefit your nervous system but learning to regulate your nervous system "manually" can also improve healing.
- The amygdala, a part of the brain associated with emotional processing, is often hyperactive in individuals with PTSD. This heightened reactivity contributes to increased emotional responses, particularly fear and anxiety. Therapeutic interventions involving the nervous system can actually readjust the amygdala's responses.
- In addition, healing can support the hippocampus—a region involved in memory processing and contextualizing experiences—in processing and integrating traumatic memories, allowing for a more adaptive response to reminders of the trauma.
- Healing can also promote neuroplasticity thanks to the role of the nervous system. Neuroplasticity refers to the brain's ability to reorganize itself by forming new neural connections. Trauma and stress can lead to both structural and functional changes in the brain, but healing involves promoting neuroplasticity to rewire maladaptive neural circuits and enhance resilience.

As you can see, the nervous system has a heavy hand in how trauma and healing function. With that understanding, you can move forward with a rock-solid appreciation for the body and strategic knowledge for making big splashes when it comes to amplifying your healing journey.

Recognizing Trauma Responses

Trauma responses are another key element that you have to consider when it comes to trauma and the body. Now, we take a look at what trauma responses are and how you can succinctly identify your own.

What is a Trauma Response?

A trauma response is a psychological, emotional, or physical response that you may experience in response to an event or situation that reminds you of a traumatic event. Trauma responses are often automatic and can manifest in a variety of ways, impacting thoughts, emotions, and behaviors.

In order to successfully overcome the impacts of your trauma in daily life, you have to actually know those responses and how they influence you. Some common trauma responses include:

- **Hyperarousal**: Hyperarousal can be identified by increased alertness, irritability, difficulty concentrating, hypervigilance, exaggerated startle response, and a heightened state of anxiety. Many people are triggered into a state of hyperarousal by loud noises, crowded spaces, or situations reminiscent of the traumatic event.

- **Hypoarousal**: Different from hyperarousal, hypoarousal involves feeling detached, numbness, disorientation, a sense of unreality, and a desire to withdraw or avoid stimuli. People commonly experience this due to situations that remind them of traumatic experiences, emotional overwhelm, or sensory overload.
- **Flashbacks**: A flashback involves vivid and intrusive memories of the traumatic event, feeling as if the trauma is happening again, or a loss of connection to the present moment, including environmental cues, sounds, smells, or situations reminiscent of the traumatic experience.
- **Avoidance**: Another trauma response is avoidance, which involves steering clear of situations, people, or places that remind the individual of the trauma, often to prevent emotional distress. Specific locations, activities, or individuals associated with the traumatic event can trigger avoidance.
- **Emotional dysregulation**: Intense mood swings; difficulty managing emotions; and feelings of anger, sadness, or fear that seem disproportionate to the current situation characterize emotional dysregulation, which is often triggered by stressful situations, reminders of the trauma, or interpersonal conflicts.
- **Hyperventilation**: Hyperventilation involves rapid or shallow breathing, feeling lightheaded, and experiencing physical symptoms of anxiety. This can be prompted by various stimuli, including anxiety-provoking situations, memories of the trauma, or situations that feel threatening.

At the same time, trauma responses and triggers can look different for each person, which underscores the importance of being able to identify your own trauma responses and triggers.

Identifying Trauma Responses and Triggers

Somatic therapy can help you identify your trauma responses and triggers, but it helps if you go into the practice with an idea of what responses you'd like to conquer. Here are some common and unparalleled methods for identifying your personal trauma responses:

- **Self-reflection**: Reflecting upon your physical and emotional experiences can be helpful and increase self-awareness. Consider what you were doing just before you experienced a drastic change in mood or a trauma response and you'll know what triggered you.
- **Therapeutic support**: Therapy, even self-guided, can help you achieve a more profound understanding of your own trauma responses.
- **Psychoeducation**: Understanding the interconnection of the mind-body connection and the influences of the world around you will empower you to manage your responses to stress, trauma, and triggers more effectively.
- **Mindfulness**: Incorporate mindfulness techniques, such as deep breathing or grounding exercises, to help you stay present and manage overwhelming sensations or emotions.

- **Safety plan**: Develop a safety plan that includes identifying triggers, coping strategies, and a support network.

The body is like a piggy bank for traumatic experiences, collecting them like loose change until you break it open and examine what's inside. With that being said, now that you understand how the body and trauma intertwine, as well as how somatic therapy impacts the mind-body connection circling trauma, it's time to truly begin the somatic therapy experience, starting with preparation.

CHAPTER 3:
PREPARING FOR SOMATIC PRACTICE

Healing requires from us to stop struggling, but to enjoy life more and endure it less.

—Darina Stoyanova

With your foundational knowledge, you now understand what somatic therapy is and how trauma influences the body (in turn, this allows for knowledge regarding how somatic therapy can improve body-related trauma symptoms). Now it's time to dive into how you can prepare for somatic therapy. Many people try to skip this stage, but I want to caution you against that; preparation is vital for a safe and comfortable experience. In this chapter, you will master simple yet effective ways to prepare your setting, mindset, and self for the experience of somatic therapy.

Creating a Safe Space for Practice

Creating a safe space for your somatic therapy practice is vital. Somatic therapy—and any therapy, really—can unearth some rather uncomfortable feelings, sensations, and memories. The work you do will be easier to consolidate and appreciate if it is done in an environment that is safe and comfortable. With that being said, what can you do to make a safe space for your somatic therapy journey?

Designing Your Therapeutic Environment

Creating a safe therapeutic environment that feels secure and private includes considering various elements. For example, you'll always want to pick a space that's both quiet and private. You don't want to be interrupted while you're in the middle of a session, and it's helpful if you have no onlookers as well. Make use of curtains, blinds, or strategically placing items to give you some privacy as you work.

In addition, it's helpful if you take a look at lighting. Soft yet natural lighting can be best for somatic therapy practices, especially because vitamin D and the natural light that carries it can positively impact mood. However, if you are unable to make use of natural light or prefer something different, you can make use of adjustable lighting options. Candles and fairy lights, for instance, can create a peaceful and warm ambiance.

I also recommend that you have a comfortable place to sit, even if you plan to sit on the floor. A comfortable chair, cushion, or mat to sit or even lie down on can make sessions better. Moreover, proper body support is necessary to allow your body to relax and empower you to focus on the therapeutic process (as opposed to your physical discomfort from sitting somewhere uncomfortable).

Being mindful of the ambiance and decor in your therapeutic area can be helpful too. Calming colors and personal items that bring you peace, for instance, can make the area more inviting. Consider using items like blankets, pillows, or soft textures to create a cozy and inviting atmosphere. You can also take advantage of scents from oils and incense to enhance the setting. Don't be afraid to make it your own!

At the same time, it's good to work in an organized area. Keeping the space tidy can help you avoid distractions or lose your train of thought as you work on your healing journey. You should also grab some storage options for things like pens, paper, workbooks, and more to keep your therapeutic supplies organized and nearby and minimize searching for them and clutter.

Your therapeutic space can also be amplified with natural elements and sensory experiences. Even a singular potted plant can bring some life and comfort to the room. Soft, calming, or natural background music can work to subtly calm you down as you work through tougher emotions. It's also a wonderful idea to include soft physical elements, like pillows and rugs, so that you can make use of and feel comfortable in the entire room.

Temperature control is another big element of personalizing and designing your therapeutic space. Extreme temperatures can be distracting, so be sure to set the thermostat to your perfect setting before sitting down for therapy. Oh, and keep a blanket nearby—sometimes regulation due to relaxation exercises can leave you a bit chilly.

Finally, try to avoid inviting electronics into the therapeutic space. While you might use a device for music or a guided meditation, try not to look at screens or let loud notification sounds catch you off guard as you work. A pre-therapy digital detox can do wonders for boosting the benefits of your session.

It might sound like I'm implying that in order to work with self-guided somatic therapy, you need a fancy office space with a bunch of new furniture. That isn't the case at all; somatic therapy can be done in a bedroom, your living room, or even the hallway closet provided that you have enough space. The most important thing is to personalize that environment and minimize distractions or discomfort where possible.

Personal Boundaries and Consent

In a clinical setting, there is something called informed consent that drives the practice of many professionals. It involves disclosing anything to the patient before doing it with them, such as letting them know that a medication the professional plans to prescribe is experimental. Informed consent is important because it lets patients decide whether they can handle something before it is sprung onto them. So why am I telling you this if you're your own therapist?

It's because you have to get your *own* informed consent before engaging with a practice. Right now, you are still learning about the ins and outs of somatic therapy, so you cannot truly gather your own informed consent. In order to do so, it's important that you learn as much as you can—both by reading this book and by checking out other resources relevant to questions you may need answered—before considering your consent to be informed.

Once you feel ready to dive into actually practicing informed consent and somatic therapy, make sure that you set an intention. You can pick an intention that's just a single word or even draw up a contract with yourself. This helps you understand what you hope to get out of each individual session or out of your therapeutic practice as a whole. Something like "I, [name], will practice somatic therapy with the intention of [goal], keeping in mind that [boundaries, risks, and limits]" works as a personal contract. For instance, "I, Jane, will practice somatic therapy for healing my trauma responses, keeping in mind that I may find discomfort and anxiety during the process" is a good intention.

For anyone self-guiding the process of somatic therapy, it's also important that you set boundaries and guidelines for your practice. While somatic therapy is safe and pushing yourself can be wonderful, you don't want to go too far. You should set guidelines and personal boundaries regarding

- what you will and will not try (either for now or long-term)
- signs that you should stop or work with grounding/relaxation methods
- topics that you do and do not want to cover initially
- anything else that comes to mind regarding keeping yourself safe and comfortable during somatic therapy.

As you can probably tell, it's important to educate yourself regarding somatic therapy before you delve into its practices. At the same time, I also suggest that you have a support network that you can turn to if you need comfort, reassurance, or guidance regarding where to go next with your journey.

Furthermore, it's important that you create a relationship of trust with yourself before you begin and during your early experiences with self-guided somatic therapy. Trusting yourself means ensuring that you know that you have your best interest at heart, as well as that it's okay to be vulnerable with yourself.

Trusting yourself throughout the therapeutic process can begin with something like self-care. For example, tending to your emotional and physical needs can help you understand, even on a subconscious level, that you're a safe and encouraging person to be around. This means that it's vital to care for your needs as a part of the process of learning to trust yourself. After all, you want to trust your therapist.

Self-Compassion and Emotional Safety

The final aspect of creating a safe space for your practice that you need to be aware of is engaging with self-compassion and empathy. Self-compassion is incredibly important, especially in the context of a therapeutic space. With self-compassion, you can handle troubling emotions and roadblocks with resilience and efficiency. Here are some ways that you can cultivate self-compassion during the process of self-guided somatic therapy:

- **Comfort yourself**: In the face of particularly strong or overwhelming emotions, be sure to be kind to yourself and comfort yourself. You can hone self-comfort skills through learning grounding, relaxation, and self-soothing tactics.
- **Be mindful**: Being mindful can help you maintain presence and awareness when it comes to your emotions. When it comes to more challenging emotions, being mindful can help you be aware of how those emotions influence you and how you respond to them.
- **Practice acceptance**: Many people try to force their emotions down or away. By practicing acceptance, however, you become kinder to yourself by recognizing that there are no "good" or "bad" emotions—they're just emotions.
- **What would you say to a friend?**: You can also promote self-compassion in your life by asking yourself what you would say to a friend in the same situation. We are often much harsher to ourselves than we would be to others.

Additionally, you have to create an atmosphere of emotional safety and empathy by acknowledging and validating your feelings. When you feel fear, anger, sadness, or any other emotion, it might be tempting to tell yourself that you shouldn't feel a certain way—that's not true and such a mindset actively holds you back.

Rather than pushing your emotions away, you have to accept them. Let yourself accept that it's alright to feel things, explore your emotions, and understand how you feel. By accepting what you feel and even validating your emotions—through letting yourself have permission to feel them—you can get further with your somatic therapy. Remember that the point of somatic therapy is to recover, which you cannot do without getting in touch with your emotions.

The attitude that you should have going into somatic therapy is one of non-judgment. You shouldn't judge your emotions as either good or bad, instead accepting that they just are. Non-judgment can be cultivated through mindfulness, awareness, and patience with yourself. If you catch yourself judging how you feel about your emotions, thoughts, or experiences, try to remind yourself that everyone experiences uncomfortable aspects of life, and it's no reason to judge yourself.

The Importance of Grounding

Grounding is one of the foundational and essential skills that you need in order to begin your somatic therapy experience. It is because of grounding that you are able to feel present and aware during your experience. Grounding also ensures that the process of somatic therapy is safe for your mental and physiological health.

Understanding Grounding for Self-Guided Practice

Grounding is a technique used both in and outside of therapy, but it also has specific uses in the context of somatic therapy. Within somatic therapy, grounding is used to help individuals connect with the present moment, their bodies, and the environment around them. In the context of self-guided somatic therapy, grounding plays a crucial role in managing emotional responses, especially when dealing with triggers or overwhelming sensations.

Grounding techniques can assist in creating a sense of safety and stability, allowing you to navigate and process emotions more effectively. Grounding techniques are particularly valuable when it comes to managing triggers. Once you identify and isolate a trigger or trauma response, you can then use grounding techniques to bring attention to the resulting physical sensations. It allows you to connect back with your physical body and the present moment, rather than becoming intensely aware of the traumatic experiences in your memory.

Grounding techniques can also help you manage emotional responses and control overwhelming feelings during the process of self-guided treatment. This means that grounding will give you the opportunity to safely work through some of the more challenging or exhausting facets of your trauma while still remaining, for the most part, comfortable.

Some people believe that grounding is a one-size-fits-all approach, but that couldn't be farther from the truth. With the right knowledge of grounding and a few key considerations, you can make grounding work for your unique needs and preferences:

- **Breathing exercises**: Grounding is heavy on using breathing exercises as a tool to bring you back to reality; however, you are free to experiment with breathing exercises, modifying them and picking the ones that work best for you.
- **Sensory grounding**: You can also work with different grounding techniques that fit your preferences. If mindfulness or breathing is too abstract for you, you can work with sensory grounding. This can involve holding onto a textured object, feeling the texture of a surface, smelling a calming scent, or listening to soothing music or sounds.
- **Movement and body awareness**: Gentle movements and elements of bodily awareness can be incorporated for a present-focused approach that anchors you physically.
- **Visualization**: Visualizing or creating a mental safe space can give you an internally calming environment that you can return to in order to ground yourself, especially if real life feels less than secure.
- **Affirmations and self-talk**: Some people ground better by talking to themselves. You can incorporate affirmations like "I am present" to help you remain grounded through speech and hearing.
- **Nature**: You also have the option to ground yourself through nature, connecting with natural elements either by heading outside or bringing nature into your space. There are even studies that link digging your hands into soil with enhanced dopamine and grounding!

- **Mindful observation**: Another tool that you can use to customize your experience is mindful observation—simply take note of the small parts of your environment that you would normally overlook.

As you personalize your experience with grounding, it's a good idea to create a "grounding toolkit," a list of the techniques that work best for you. Even if you think you can remember them, creating a toolkit list can actually help you make grounding a routine an automatic practice, setting your somatic therapy sessions off right each and every time.

Tailoring Grounding Practices to Your Lifestyle

When I tell people that grounding is an instrumental aspect of preparing for a somatic therapy session, many people groan or roll their eyes. To them, grounding is boring or an inconvenience, something that they understand in theory but loathe in practice. I understand that—if I was working with a set of practices that were not attuned to my personal needs, convenient for my lifestyle, or otherwise helpful to me personally, I wouldn't want to do it either.

Rather than condemning the practice of grounding—which has scientific benefits and is proven to have a positive benefit on somatic therapy—try making an effort to tailor grounding practices to your lifestyle. When it comes to therapeutic and mental health practices, you are *allowed* to change things to make them easier and more accessible to you, and that includes grounding.

For instance, you're allowed and able to make grounding a comforting experience. Something as simple as lighting a candle and being mindful of that candle with all four senses (barring taste, of course)—what does it look like, smell like, how is the heat of the flame radiating, can you hear a crackle—can be a grounding exercise. This plays to the senses, which is a quick and comfortable yet effective way to ground for many people.

You can also include various physical items into your grounding system. For example, some people find that fidget toys like spinners, clickers, and popping toys are able to ground them. Not only do these objects serve as sensory input, but holding onto an object can be a grounding experience. Don't be afraid to include comforting items that help you begin or explore grounding for somatic therapy.

And while technology may not make the best addition to a somatic therapy session, you can certainly use it for elements of grounding—whether that be getting into the habit of grounding or guiding you in grounding before each session. Apps like Mind or Headspace include grounding meditations, or you can search for them on YouTube. Such meditations include a speaker that will let you know how to ground yourself in a relaxed tone. You can also use music, metronomes, or other tools to ground you, all thanks to the powers of technology.

You also have the ability to make grounding more convenient or fit into your routine. Grounding doesn't have to happen strictly before a somatic therapy experience; by patterning your life with elements of grounding, you can enhance your mental presence and the benefits of your therapeutic practices. Here are some options for time-effective grounding:

- **Eating**: How many meals do you have when you're completely zoned out? Try paying attention to your food and the experience of eating with all five senses. You already eat, so this is a nice way to add in some mindfulness and grounding.
- **Driving**: Grounding during driving or another form of commuting is as simple as engaging with the environment with all five senses. Allow yourself to find brief opportunities for grounding and an appreciation for the world around you during such transitional periods.
- **Nature**: When you find yourself in nature, even if for just a few moments, find the opportunity to ground yourself. Let yourself feel how stable the ground is beneath you or pay attention to the sway of the leaves from the breeze.
- **Chores**: No one likes washing the dishes, but it's a sensory experience that gifts you the opportunity to ground during the busy tide of your day.

As you can see, grounding yourself doesn't have to confirm to strictly traditional techniques. It doesn't even have to be like the tools mentioned in this book, so long as the practice is effective for you!

Maintaining Connection With Your Body

During a self-guided somatic therapy session, one of the most important considerations is remaining mentally and physically connected with your body. After all, somatic therapy is the most body-centered therapy tactic, so it's important to remain in touch with your bodily experiences throughout a session. Grounding is a powerful tool for bodily awareness. Typically, we lose awareness of our bodies as our heads enter the clouds; drawing those thoughts back to the present almost always involves some element of body awareness.

Therefore, I cannot highlight the importance enough—ensure that your grounding tactics have a body-focused element so that you can return awareness to the sensations and experiences of the body. This is pivotal to empowering yourself through somatic therapy, as this awareness allows you to really tune in to how your trauma presents through the body, even when the mind doesn't know it.

Breathing Techniques for Centering and Focus

The final major preparatory tactic for somatic therapy is breathing and breathing techniques that can help you remain centered and focused. When it comes to the mind, being centered involves bringing the mind to a state where it can focus solely on the task at hand. Many spiritual practitioners, for example, center before engaging with their practices so that mundane tasks or concerns don't interfere. Naturally, this improves the efficacy of something like somatic therapy.

Conscious Breathing for Self-Centering

Breathing serves as a pioneer in self-centering tactics and the cultivation of present-moment awareness. The act of intentional breathing brings attention to the current moment, fostering a connection between the mind and body. It serves as an anchor, allowing you to ground yourself in the present and navigate through somatic experiences.

There are hundreds of breathing exercises that you can engage in. Some of my favorite—and the most effective—breathing exercises, alongside their instructions, are as follows:

- 4-7-8 breathing
    - Inhale quietly through your nose for a count of 4.
    - Hold your breath for a count of 7.
    - Exhale completely through your mouth for a count of 8.
    - Repeat this cycle for several breaths.
- Box breathing
    - Inhale slowly for a count of 4.
    - Hold your breath for a count of 4.
    - Exhale slowly for a count of 4.
    - Pause before inhaling again, repeat the cycle.
- Alternate nostril breathing
    - Close one nostril with your thumb and inhale through the other nostril.

- Close the opposite nostril with your finger, exhale through the first nostril.
- Continue this alternate pattern, focusing on the breath and the sensation of airflow.

The Relationship Between Intentional Breathing and a Deeper Connection With Yourself

Intentional breathing is a profound way to access a deeper connection with yourself, both in and outside of the somatic therapy experience. It enhances your awareness of the connection between the mind and body, allowing you to observe your physical and emotional world without judgment. This also leads to enhanced emotional regulation, balancing the aspects of the nervous system in the process.

Incorporating intentional breathing into your self-guided somatic therapy practice provides a valuable and accessible means of fostering self-awareness, emotional regulation, and a more profound connection with yourself. Experiment with different techniques to find what resonates best with you and make conscious breathing a regular part of your somatic therapy routine.

Exploring Breathwork Practices

Breathwork practices can be simple or complex. In the last section, I introduced you to three fundamental breathwork practices. Now, let's engage with three more slightly more challenging breathwork practices that can improve physical awareness and provide you with a deep sense of comfort and centering:

- Diaphragmatic breathing
  - Sit or lie down comfortably.
  - Inhale slowly through your nose, allowing your diaphragm to expand.
  - Exhale slowly through your mouth, feeling your belly contract.
  - Focus on the rise and fall of your abdomen with each breath.
  - Repeat for several breaths.
- Paced breathing
  - Inhale and exhale for an equal count (i.e., inhale for a count of 4, exhale for a count of 4).
  - Gradually increase the count as you become comfortable.
  - Maintain a smooth, rhythmic flow of breath.
  - Experiment with different inhale-exhale ratios to find what feels most calming.
- Ujjayi breathing (ocean breath)
  - Inhale slowly through your nose, slightly constricting the back of your throat.
  - Exhale through your nose with the same slight constriction, creating a soft "ocean-like" sound.
  - This technique can help bring a sense of calm and focus.

Understanding How Breathwork Contributes to Emotional Regulation and Stress Reduction

When you engage with breathwork, the deep and intentional motions of the process stimulate your parasympathetic nervous system. This soothes the mind and body and promotes relaxation that can soothe your "fight or flight" response. In this way, breathing enhances your emotional regulation by creating a pause between a stimulus and your response. This helps you approach situations with greater calmness and clarity.

In addition, mindful breathing has been linked to lower levels of cortisol, a hormone that is elevated when you face stress. This can contribute to an overall reduction in stress and anxiety. Overall, breathing not only improves stress, but your focus, presence, and quality of somatic therapy benefits.

Creating a Breath-Focused Ritual

Establishing a personal breathwork routine and ritual is simple and can amplify your practice. There are some steps that you can take advantage of for establishing a personalized breath-focused ritual:

1. **Set an intention**: Begin your ritual by setting an intention for your somatic therapy session. This could be focused on relaxation, self-awareness, or emotional regulation.
2. **Comfortable space**: Choose a quiet and comfortable space where you will not be disturbed. Create

an environment that supports relaxation, perhaps with soft lighting or calming elements.

3. **Seated or comfortable posture**: Find a comfortable seated or lying-down position. Ensure that your spine is straight, allowing for optimal breath flow.
4. **Begin with breath awareness**: Start by bringing awareness to your natural breath. Observe the rhythm, depth, and sensation of each inhale and exhale.
5. **Incorporate diaphragmatic breathing**: Transition into diaphragmatic breathing. Inhale deeply through your nose, allowing your diaphragm to expand. Exhale slowly through your mouth, feeling your belly contract.
6. **Combine with movement**: Integrate gentle movements that align with your breath. For example, raise your arms overhead as you inhale and lower them as you exhale. Coordinate the movement with your breath to enhance the mind-body connection.
7. **Visualization technique**: Incorporate visualization into your breath-focused ritual. Imagine inhaling positive energy or light, and as you exhale, visualize releasing tension, stress, or negative emotions.
8. **Create a flow**: Develop a flow that combines breath awareness, diaphragmatic breathing, movement, and visualization. Allow each element to seamlessly transition into the next, creating a harmonious and integrated practice.

9. **Set a duration**: Determine the length of your breath-focused ritual based on your preferences and the time available. This could range from a few minutes to longer sessions, depending on your needs.

They might seem like small practices, but the benefits of everything mentioned within this chapter stack up, empowering you to have a successful somatic therapy sessions where you feel confident and safe. Before moving on to the next chapters, which highlight somatic therapy techniques, be sure that you're comfortable with yourself, with grounding, and with centering and focus to maximize somatic benefits.

CHAPTER 4: SOMATIC EXERCISES- PART 1: AWARENESS

Our sorrows and wounds are healed only when we touch them with compassion.

—Buddha

So you're ready for somatic therapy... what now? It all begins with awareness. Because somatic therapy involves understanding how trauma presents in the body through the mind-body connection and awareness, you have to actually begin with somatic therapy exercises and techniques that hone your ability to be aware. That's what this chapter is all about!

Body Scanning for Awareness and Relaxation

Body scanning is an unparalleled tactic for awareness and relaxation. Body scanning involves bringing awareness to different areas of the body, which is naturally incredibly beneficial for finding places where trauma may be stored through pain, discomfort, or sensation-based memory. In this section, you will unlock the secrets to body scanning for awareness and relaxation. Let's jump in!

Introduction to Body Scanning

Body scanning is a foundational practice within somatic therapy. It involves directing your focused attention systematically toward various parts of the body, observing and becoming aware of physical sensations, tensions, and emotions. This practice is designed to enhance self-awareness, promote relaxation, and facilitate a deeper connection between the mind and body.

As a key component of self-guided somatic therapy, body scanning can help you understand your bodily experiences and learn to release tensions and traumas. Let's look at a few of the benefits of body scanning:

- **Enhanced self-awareness**: Body scanning is powerful when it comes to increasing your awareness of bodily sensations, thus deepening the mind-body connection. Such awareness can help you understand your physiological states more completely.
- **Stress reduction**: Due to the systematic scanning nature of a body scan, you can consciously release and relax stress and pain in specific area. This can highlight stress reduction benefits while also making it less strenuous to observe problem areas.
- **Mind-body connection**: Body scanning provides you with a multifaceted understanding of how the mind and body are connected, as well as how emotional states can manifest in a physical sense.
- **Emotional regulation**: If your body is the landscape that your emotions reside within, then body

scanning is the technique that allows you to excavate and explore them. You can look at your emotions and accept them, ultimately working toward regulating and transforming your emotional experiences.

- **Mindfulness**: Body scanning is a mindfulness practice that helps you stay in the moment and avoid judgment. This mindful awareness can extend beyond the practice into daily life.
- **Tension release**: The systematic scanning of the body allows for the identification and release of tension. By bringing attention to tense areas, you can consciously relax those muscles, promoting a sense of ease and comfort and potentially working on letting go of certain traumas.

Particularly, we want to focus on how body scanning empowers you to let go of tension and stress—two of the biggest manifestations of trauma in the body. Body scanning helps identify and manage tension and stress because it allows you to identify different parts of the body that may be holding significant or disproportionate levels of stress or tension—often signifying a traumatic store. For instance, you might find that an area impacted by an assault still hurts or holds tension.

As you bring awareness to individual parts of the body, you can consciously relax them, contributing to a mental and physical release. Delving more into release tactics will also be covered in Chapter 5. Between mindful, conscious reaction and breathing integration, you can support body scanning in a way that makes somatic therapy easier than ever.

Step-by-Step Body Scanning Techniques

Body scanning is a valuable practice for somatic therapy because it truly highlights the hallmark mind-body connection. The basic steps to body scanning are as follows:

1. Find a cozy spot where you can enjoy some quiet time alone.
2. Get comfortable, whether sitting or lying down. Make sure you're well-supported and simply let yourself relax.
3. Start by turning your focus to your breath. Breathe in deep and slow, feeling your chest fill up, and then exhale, letting go of any tension. Embrace the calm.
4. Approach the body scan with a relaxed and curious attitude. Let go of judgments and flow with the sensations without categorizing them. No need for good or bad labels.
5. Direct your attention to your toes, the starting point. Observe whatever is happening—warmth, coolness, or a bit of tension. Take a leisurely scan through each toe.
6. Gradually shift your focus down to the soles of your feet, exploring every inch, from the bottom to the top. Acknowledge any sensations, whether tension or a gentle release.
7. Move your attention upward, acknowledging your ankles, and then explore the sensations in your

calves. Feel into these areas, recognizing any subtle feelings or impressions.

8. Continue your upward journey, traveling through your knees and up into your thighs. Take a deliberate pause at each section, immersing yourself in the sensations that unfold.
9. Guide your awareness to your pelvis and hips. Feel into this region, acknowledging any tightness, warmth, or comforting ease.
10. Shift your attention to your lower back, upper back, and abdomen. Connect with your breath and notice the sensations in these vital areas.
11. Direct your awareness to your chest and shoulders. Observe the rhythmic rise and fall of your chest with each breath. Tune into any feelings of tension or ease.
12. Extend your focus down your arms, from the shoulders to the fingertips. Feel the sensations, whether it's a gentle warmth, tingling, or a subtle awareness in your hands.
13. Guide your attention to the neck, a bridge between the upper and lower body. Feel into this area, noting any sensations of tightness or the softening of muscles.
14. Finally, bring your awareness to your head and face. Explore the sensations in your scalp, forehead, eyes, cheeks, and jaw. Take your time to fully immerse yourself in each area.
15. After completing the scan, take a moment to reconnect with your breath. Observe how your body feels as a unified whole, appreciating the subtle shifts and releases that may have occurred.

16. Reflect on your experience with a compassionate and open mind. Acknowledge any insights, changes in sensations, or discoveries of tension. Embrace the practice without passing judgment on what unfolded.

Beginners might struggle with body scanning or understanding what to do. Don't worry; with time and practice, the process becomes easier. For now, focus on going at your own pace. You don't need to rush through something as instrumental as a body scan. Instead, slow down and take your time to notice the sensations in your body. At the same time, if a guided audio or something similar goes so slowly you're becoming bored or falling asleep, don't be afraid to speed it up—so long as you're still dedicating enough time to each body part.

Additionally, it helps if you go into and consider the process with a curious, non-judgmental mindset. Allow yourself to be curious about the different processes and sensations that you're uncovering, diving into each body part with the same level of compassion each time. Try to avoid putting labels on each part, instead opting to observe. For example, instead of thinking that your hip holds a lot of negative emotions and energy, consider it in terms of the way your hip holds a lot of built up emotions or trauma-related pains.

It's more important to be consistent with a practice like this than it is to be perfect. Even if you feel like nothing happened or was revealed during your first body scan, allow it to become a consistent part of your routine. Not only is it relaxing and soothing, but it can, over time, empower you to become more aware—eventually revealing those hidden aspects to you.

Also remember that you have the power to customize your body scanning experience. For instance, if someone in a recording that you chose moves from one part to the next too fast, or you want to spend longer with one part of the body, you have the ability to customize that and allocate your time differently. At the end of the day, your practice should benefit *you*, regardless of what a recording says.

Body Scanning Variations and Adaptations

Body scanning doesn't have to look the same for everyone. Some people will encourage you to body scan in certain positions or certain ways, but you don't have to match those requests at all. In fact, there are many body scanning variations and adaptations that you can make use of:

- **Mindful movement**: Combine body scanning with gentle movements. Flow through the scan while incorporating stretches or yoga poses, synchronizing each movement with your breath.
- **Seated**: Practice body scanning in a seated position if lying down isn't suitable. Keep your spine straight and focus on each body part, maintaining a mindful awareness of sensations.
- **Walking**: Extend body scanning to a walking meditation. Pay attention to each step, gradually moving

your awareness from your toes to the top of your head.

- **Expressive**: Allow your body to express itself during the scan. If a particular body part feels tense, explore gentle movements or stretches to release tension.
- **Quick focus**: Adapt the body scan to fit shorter time frames. Rapidly scan through key areas, focusing on the most tension-prone regions, allowing for a brief yet effective practice.
- **Progressive**: Systematically divide the body into segments for different sessions. Focus on specific regions during each practice, creating a progressive and thorough exploration over time.

You can also adapt body scanning for different abilities, time constraints, and other needs. You can include micro-body scans into your routine, for instance. This can be accommodating for time-based needs as well as various attention deficits. You can also opt to stand and do a body scan if you're in no position to sit or lay, and you can even integrate body scanning alongside posture improvement. Customizing the practice helps you get more out of it while simultaneously encouraging you to engage with it.

Mindful Movement Exercises

In Chapter 1, I discussed how somatic therapy often involves using movement to determine where in the body trauma is held, as well as to incite healing. Now, it's time to really dig into how those mindful movements can improve your somatic therapy experience, especially through mindful movement exercises.

Understanding Mindful Movement

Mindful movement is a practice that involves bringing your attention to the present moment while engaging with physical, movement-based activities. It combines the principles of mindfulness with purposeful movement, emphasizing a conscious and non-judgmental presence during the experience. Mindful movement is particularly helpful for somatic therapy, as it encourages you to fully engage your senses, thoughts, and emotions in the unfolding movement, fostering a deep connection between the mind and the body.

Mindful movement has a particularly important role when it comes to cultivating awareness and presence. It shifts the external distractions out of focus, instead highlighting the experience of the body in motion and the associated sensations. As a result, one gains a heightened awareness of their bodily sensations, movements, and surroundings.

During the process of mindful movement, you have to deliberately tune into the body's actions, the rhythm of breath, and the sensations that arise. A state of non-judgment must be achieved, allowing you to observe both your body's capabilities and limitations with ease. With a mindset free from criticism, you can create a space for self-acceptance and a more compassionate relationship with your body. In turn, this empowers you to have an open relationship where you can address challenges and obstacles.

In addition, practicing mindful movement with regularity deepens your ability to be mindfully aware. As you become attuned to the subtle movements and sensations of the body, you gain a more profound understanding of its system. Moreover, mindful movement is perfect for the context of somatic therapy because it emphasizes the integration of mind and body. The awareness cultivated during movement extends beyond physical actions, influencing mental and emotional states. This holistic integration enhances overall well-being.

The Connection Between Movement and the Somatic Experience

In specific, there are countless ways that mindful movement can benefit the somatic experience as a therapeutic practice:

- **Somatic exploration**: Mindful movement is a gateway that leads to somatic exploration, helping you to dive into the sensory experiences of your body. This involves paying attention to internal sensations, emotions, and the body's responses to different movements.
- **Release of tension**: Through mindful movement, you can identify areas of tension and explore ways to release it. The conscious engagement with the somatic experience during movement provides an opportunity for tension to be acknowledged and alleviated.

- **Emotional expression**: Mindful movement is a phenomenal form of emotional expression, allowing you to connect with and express your emotions through gestures, postures, and the flow of your movements.
- **Mind-body dialogue**: Perhaps most importantly, mindful movement opens up a mind-body dialogue. The intentional connection between mental focus and physical action fosters a reciprocal relationship, where each informs and influences the other, creating a dynamic and integrated experience.

It is thanks to these benefits that we can recognize the power of mindful movement when it comes to enhancing the experience of somatic therapy.

Guided Mindful Movement Sequences

Now that you understand the value of mindful movement when it comes to self-guided somatic therapy, you're probably wondering how you can actually engage with such a thing. It is as simple as engaging with some mindful movement sequences, such as the following activities:

- **Breath awareness and arm circles**: Stand or sit comfortably. Inhale, lifting your arms out to the sides and up overhead. Exhale, bringing them down in a circular motion. Coordinate each breath with a full circle, fostering awareness of your breath and the movement of your arms. Repeat for one to two minutes.

- **Seated forward fold with breathing**: Sit comfortably on the floor or in a chair. Inhale, lengthening your spine. Exhale, hinging at your hips, and gently fold forward. Allow your breath to guide the movement, inhaling as you lengthen and exhaling as you fold. Hold for a few breaths and return to an upright position.
- **Mindful walking**: Take a slow walk, paying attention to each step. Inhale for a certain number of steps, and exhale for the same number. Notice the sensation in your feet as they lift and touch the ground. This simple walking exercise enhances both breath awareness and mindful movement.
- **Gentle neck stretches**: Sit or stand comfortably. Inhale, lengthening your spine. Exhale, tilting your head to one side, feeling a gentle stretch along your neck. Inhale back to center, and exhale to the opposite side. Repeat for several breath cycles, moving slowly and with intention.
- **Body scanning in motion**: Stand with feet hip-width apart. Inhale, raising your arms overhead. Exhale, bringing your hands down, and slowly bend forward, allowing your spine to articulate. Inhale as you rise, stacking each vertebra. Connect each movement with your breath, creating a flowing, body-scan-like sequence.
- **Seated twist with breathing**: Sit comfortably with your spine tall. Inhale, lengthening your spine. Exhale, gently twisting to one side. Inhale back to the center, and exhale to the other side. Coordinate the

breath with the movement, focusing on the gentle twist and the expansion of your ribcage.
- **Mindful stretching**: Stand or sit comfortably. Inhale, reaching your arms overhead. Exhale, leaning to one side, feeling a stretch along your torso. Inhale back to the center, and exhale to the opposite side. Focus on the breath and the sensations of stretching. Repeat for several cycles.

In order to have a mindful and embodied practice, it's also important to ground and center before your session. Set an intention before you engage with the practice, similar to what we discussed in Chapter 3. Then, be mindful of the sensations and experiences of each individual movement throughout the entirety of your body.

Incorporating Mindful Movement Into Daily Life

We live in a busy world. Every day, the hustle and bustle of life can make it hard to take even a moment for yourself. This is when it can be helpful to understand how to incorporate mindful movement into your life, even on a daily, time-sensitive basis. You can incorporate mindful movement into your daily routines in the following ways:

- Turn your daily walks into mindful movement sessions. Pay attention to each step, the sensation of your feet on the ground, and the rhythm of your breath. This can be done during a leisurely stroll or even on your way to work.
- Take short breaks throughout the day to stretch mindfully. Whether you're at your desk or waiting

for a meeting, engage in gentle stretches like reaching overhead, twisting at the waist, or stretching your legs. Focus on the sensations and your breath.

- Transform your daily commute into a mindful experience. Whether you're driving, biking, or taking public transportation, use the time to bring awareness to your body and breath. Relax your shoulders, soften your grip, and tune into the movement or vibrations around you.
- Infuse mindfulness into household chores. Whether you're washing dishes, sweeping the floor, or folding laundry, pay attention to the movements of your body. Feel the textures, notice the scents, and use the activity as a way to center yourself in the present moment.
- Incorporate short mindful movement sessions at your desk. Perform seated stretches, neck rotations, and wrist exercises. Use the opportunity to check in with your body and release tension, promoting both physical and mental well-being.
- Pay attention to the act of eating. While seated, incorporate gentle movements like rotating your ankles, stretching your legs, or practicing seated yoga postures. This adds a mindful element to meals, fostering a connection between movement and nourishment.
- Integrate mindful breathing into moments of stillness. Whether waiting for an elevator, standing in line, or sitting at your desk, take a few conscious breaths. Inhale deeply, feeling your lungs expand, and exhale slowly, releasing any tension.

- If you encounter stairs during your day, use them as an opportunity for mindful movement. Take each step consciously, feeling the muscles engage. Use the ascent and descent as a chance to synchronize your breath with movement.
- Mindfully incorporate movement into your technology use. Stretch while watching TV, perform seated exercises during screen time, or take short breaks to stand and move around when working on a computer.
- If possible, engage in mindful movement in natural settings. Whether it's a park, garden, or your backyard, connect with the environment as you move. Engage in activities like mindful walking, gentle yoga, or simply sitting and observing nature.
- Practice mindful movement during conversations. Instead of remaining sedentary, take a walk together, engage in a light stretch, or practice grounding exercises while discussing topics. This not only promotes physical well-being but also enhances the quality of your interactions.
- During structured exercise sessions, bring a mindful approach. Pay attention to your breath, the sensations in your muscles, and the overall experience of movement. This transforms traditional workouts into mindful movement practices.
- Wind down with mindful movement before bedtime. Engage in gentle stretches or yoga poses, focusing on relaxation. This can prepare your body for restful sleep and promote a calm state of mind.

Recognizing and Understanding Body Signals

The last tactic that you need in your arsenal for somatic therapy awareness is the ability to understand your body's signals. Every day, your body signals to you that it's in pain, afraid, comfortable, stiff, or something else, and in order to heal, you need to be able to recognize these signals.

Developing Body Awareness

Understanding and being able to recognize the signals that your body gives off is invaluable in the face of somatic therapy. When you hone the ability to understand when your body is sending a signal *and* what that signal means, it becomes far easier to see and respond to what your body is trying to tell you. In the context of somatic therapy, bodily awareness helps you understand the mind-body connection and use what it's telling you to bring about an enhanced state of healing.

You see, body awareness is, at its core, an element of self-discovery. You may not be aware that an event impacted you as much as it did, yet body awareness can unlock that understanding for you. In the face of unexplained pains and inescapable anxiety, body awareness can bring you the epiphany you need in order to move forward in a proactive way that cares for your health holistically.

Furthermore, bodily awareness serves as a foundation for understanding emotions and emotional stress. If you think about it, emotions are the language of the body. Thus, you have to understand that the body is speaking in order to understand its language, meaning that understanding bodily awareness helps you decode the messages that it's sending to you.

Interpreting Sensations and Signals

Somatic therapy involves analyzing the connection between the mind and the body. For the most part, you'll have to analyze what sensations mean for your particular body; however, there are certain signals with meanings that apply to most people.

- **Tingling sensation**: This may indicate increased blood flow or heightened awareness in that area. It could also be a sign of energy movement.
- **Warmth or heat**: Often associated with increased circulation and relaxation. It might signify the release of tension.
- **Coolness**: Can suggest a calming or soothing effect on the nervous system.
- **Shallow breathing**: May indicate stress or anxiety. Bringing awareness to the breath can help regulate and deepen it.
- **Deep breathing**: Usually associated with relaxation and a parasympathetic nervous system response.
- **Tension or resistance**: Notice areas where movement feels restricted. It could reflect emotional or physical tightness that needs attention.
- **Fluid movement**: Indicates a harmonious mind-body connection. Effortless movements often coincide with a balanced emotional state.

- **Feeling rooted**: A sense of stability and connection with the ground. This can promote a feeling of safety and security.
- **Lightness or floating sensation**: Might indicate a release of stress or a shift toward a more relaxed state.

And while these are somewhat common sense, it's also important that you can tie physical responses to emotions for fulfilling interpretation:

- Shoulder and neck sensations
    - Tension or tightness: Often associated with stress, anxiety, or the need for emotional release.
    - Lightness: Feeling weight lifted off the shoulders can signal emotional relief or resolution.
- Chest sensations
    - Constriction: May reflect feelings of anxiety, fear, or emotional suppression.
    - Expansion: A sense of openness can signify emotional freedom or a release of pent-up feelings.
- Abdomen sensations
    - Butterflies or knots: Common during periods of nervousness or excitement.
    - Softening: A relaxed abdomen may coincide with emotional calmness and a sense of security.

- Jaw and face
    - Clenching or tightness: Often associated with stress, anger, or unexpressed emotions.
    - Relaxation: A softening of facial muscles can signal emotional release or a more relaxed state.
- Hands and feet sensations
    - Clenched fists or tension: May indicate feelings of frustration or the need to hold back.
    - Warmth or tingling: Suggests increased energy flow and emotional vitality.

With this information, you should look for patterns that can indicate consistent distress responses. Combine physical interpretations with emotional check-ins, especially before and after somatic practices.

Journaling and Reflective Practices

Journaling is a powerful tool that can help you become more self-aware, especially when it comes to deepening the mind-body connection. By regularly tracking and reflecting on body signals, you can gain valuable insights into your physical and emotional well-being. This practice encourages mindfulness and enhances your ability to listen to the subtle cues your body provides.

In order to get started, you're going to need a journal. You can work with online tools or a pen and paper—whichever is the most comfortable for you. Establish a consistent time for journaling, whether it's in the morning, before bed, or during specific breaks in your day. Consistency will help you notice trends and fluctuations in your mind-body connection. Then, work with some prompts like the following to help guide you:

- Describe any physical sensations or discomfort you are currently experiencing. How does your body feel at this moment?
- Connect with your emotions. What feelings are present right now, and where do you notice them in your body?
- Reflect on your recent meals. How did your body respond to different foods? Were there moments of hunger, fullness, or specific cravings?
- Explore your physical activity. How does your body feel during and after exercise? Are there particular movements that bring you joy or tension?
- Track your sleep. How well did you sleep, and did you notice any physical or emotional changes upon waking?
- Identify sources of stress throughout your day. How does your body respond to stress, and what relaxation techniques help alleviate tension?
- Take note of your breath. How are you breathing right now? Shallow or deep? Is your breath connected to your current emotional state?
- Record any self-care activities you engaged in. How did these practices impact your overall well-being and mind-body balance?

- Highlight any significant events or interactions. How did your body react to positive or challenging experiences?
- End your journaling session by expressing gratitude. What aspects of your body and mind are you thankful for today?

With your newfound tools of awareness, you can truly tap into the traumas that are being held within your body—gaining both the opportunity for profound self-awareness and connection as well as the opportunity for release. And release is what we're going to take a look at next, enabling you to release the emotions, traumas, and pains locked within your body.

CHAPTER 5: SOMATIC EXERCISES- PART 2: RELEASE

Instead of being ashamed of what you've been through, be proud of what you have overcome.

—Dr. Phil

After you gain the ability to be aware of your body and its sensations—the avenues of communication through the mind-body connection—the next step in the somatic therapy process is release. Release involves letting go of tension and pent-up emotions within the body. It doesn't mean that your trauma will magically dissipate, nor is it a one-and-done type of solution. It is through your consistent efforts that release will allow you to feel relief and power in the face of physical, body-based struggles.

Techniques for Releasing Stored Tension

When you suffer from a traumatic experience or ordeal, that trauma has to go somewhere. And while our minds hold all of our experiences in a sense, our bodies hold the resultant tension and hardship that the mind isn't sure how to disperse. Only then can we make the conscious choice to work toward releasing that tension—something possible after working with Chapter 4 for awareness. Now, it's time to examine how you can release tension stored within your body.

Introduction to Tension Release

"Big deal," you might say, "people are tense all of the time." However, there's a stark contrast between run-of-the-mill muscle tension and stored tension that is the produce of suffering. While plain old tension tends to be nothing more than a physical inconvenience, tension from trauma and experience that is stored can be a bit more significant in its impact; specifically, it can impact physical *and* mental health.

Many individuals who have a background of trauma report chronic pain due to tension and other causes. Tension in the sense we're referring to isn't necessarily *muscle* tension, but rather a sense of strain. Thus, we can see how trauma manifesting as chronic pain might be a significant strain. Moreover, the emotional tension that takes hold in a physical way can result in less care for one's body, illness, and more.

In a mental sense, such tension can be overbearing. Not only will that strain make it hard to overcome a traumatic experience, but it can also cause additional hardship—such as anxiety, PTSD, and trigger-related conflict—that make the mental strain of it all really take a toll. So when it boils down to it, tension in this regard truly is a big deal.

As tension can have significant negative effects on your mental and physical well-being, it necessarily becomes something that must be worked on in the face of self-guided somatic therapy. This tension stems from a mental source, yet manifests in a physical way. And because somatic therapy focuses primarily on how the body shows manifestations of mental pain, working with the body to alleviate that tension—both physical and metaphorical—becomes crucial.

Tension release is like cutting the cord that binds you to the trauma, pain, and other negativity that you identified in Chapter 4. It is through breathing, relaxation techniques, intentional movement, meditation, and other methods that you can truly interact with fulfilling and life-changing release that sets you free—or moves you one step closer to being free—from traumatic experience.

It is thanks to measured and controlled tension relief tactics that one can appreciate such relief in a mental and physical sense. Tension relief practices can remedy physical pains, and it can also heal your mental stress. Relaxation and stress relief from tension release can empower you to feel better *and* work through your experiences with a more positive, realistic outlook.

Breath-Centered Tension Release

One of the intentional ways that you can work to alleviate both physical and emotional tension is through breath-centered strategies. Breath-centered tension release is a holistic approach that combines mindful breathing techniques with the intention of identifying and releasing tension in both the body and mind.

During this practice, you will be able to understand and appreciate the connection between breath awareness, specific areas of tension, and the release of your physical and emotional stress. Here are some breath-centered tension release tactics that you can engage with:

- Release breaths
  - Inhale deeply, imagining you are gathering tension.
  - Hold your breath for a moment, acknowledging the tension within.
  - Exhale forcefully through your mouth and envision yourself releasing the tension.
- Bhramari Pranayama (bee breath)
  - Sit comfortably and take a deep breath in.
  - Exhale slowly while making a humming sound (like a bee).
  - Focus on the vibration and the sensation of the sound within your head.
  - Repeat for several breath cycles, allowing the soothing hum to calm your nervous system.
- Sitali Pranayama (cooling breath)
  - Curl your tongue into a tube shape or purse your lips.
  - Inhale slowly and deeply through your curled tongue or pursed lips.
  - Exhale through your nose.
  - This breath is believed to have a cooling and calming effect on the body.

You may also use any other exercises mentioned throughout the book but focus your intention on release during them. As a matter of fact, you can use *any* breathing exercise to represent breath-focused tension relief, as long as you modify it. For instance, I've modified the common "square/box breathing" method so that you can see what you might do to turn any breathing ritual into one for release:

- Original
    - Breathe in for 4 counts.
    - Hold for 4 counts.
    - Exhale for 4 counts.
    - Hold for 4 counts.
- Modified for release
    - Inhale while slowly counting to four. As you do, imagine all of the tension in your body and mind is swirling and coming together within your lungs.
    - Hold the breath inside for a 4 count as you envision the tension compacting and collecting, swirling around.
    - As you exhale for 4 counts, envision yourself forcing that tension out of your body.
    - For your final 4 count, savor the feeling of lesser tension before repeating the cycle as needed.

You can modify nearly any breathwork exercise in that fashion.

Progressive Muscle Relaxation (PMR)

Another way to not only identify physical and emotional tension stored in the body, but to release it as well, is a meditative and relaxation-based practice known as progressive muscle relaxation. Also known as PMR, progressive muscle relaxation is often recommended as a relaxation technique for anxiety and PTSD. A little known use of PMR is somatic therapy release. PMR has the ability to facilitate awareness and release in one swoop, resulting in profound interaction and connection with the body.

There are various lines of practice for how you can go about PMR, but the general steps are as follows:

1. Find a comfortable position to sit or lie down in. It's usually better to lie down, allowing the body to fully relax from head to toe. In that position, give yourself the time to relax. Breathe in and out, even working with one of the previously provided breathing techniques to relax the mind and body before you begin.
2. Start with your toes by taking your attention there. Notice any tightness or pain in your feet, continuing to breathe in and out as you focus. After taking as long as you need to notice the sensations, you're going to relax those muscles. First, clench the muscles in your feet as tight as you comfortably can, and hold for five to ten seconds. Then, release the tension.
3. Do this with every part of your body moving up from the feet, being mindful so that you don't re-

tense something you've un-tensed. You may need to do a full body repeat of PMR until you feel fully relaxed.

It might seem counterintuitive to tense your body for release, but this works for a few reasons. First, adding tension intentionally can allow your body to feel relaxed by comparison once you release the tension—thus making you feel more relaxed by comparison. In addition, PMR allows you to understand where tension was hiding through intentional tensing, highlighting what tension might feel like in different areas of the body.

PMR is most effective when you pair it with calculated breathing. In other words, as you work with PMR, your mind should be focused on two areas: breathing and bodily awareness. It's perfectly fine to just take deep, mindful breaths as you go, but don't be afraid to work with breathing exercises if you have the ability to focus on both. I recommend starting simple!

Movement Exercises for Emotional Release

Movement is another phenomenal way to release emotions that are stored in a physical sense. As you know, emotions can manifest physically and then find themselves stored within the body. Through movement and movement-related activity, you can work with releasing these emotions through forceful actions, expression, and more.

Understanding Emotional Release Through Movement

In somatic therapy, movement is both literally and representationally healing. What this means is that not only can movement empower you to overcome physical manifestations, but it can also be used to produce physical representations of inward emotions. This can help you understand and move through troubling feelings that come up over the course of somatic therapy.

In addition, it's important to understand that movement naturally helps the body move through experiences. A somatic therapist would, for instance, encourage you to physically represent anger as you work through anger. By outwardly expressing anger by doing something like clenching your fists, you may be more aware of emotions or specific factors that accompany anger—thus enabling you to release those emotions.

Therefore, the connection between movement and emotional catharsis becomes apparent. Think about a ballet dancer who beautifully uses their body to communicate sorrow, passion, or pride. Their body becomes a catalyst for outward expression *and* release of such emotions, hinting at by the fact that many people view dance—even as a sport—as cathartic. Similarly, movement can help you express and release built up or stored emotions.

In order for your movement-based release to be fruitful, it's important that you go into the process with an attitude of non-judgment. It can be easy to judge your body on its appearance, ability, or actions—or even for experiencing pain and trauma—but these judgments aren't helpful. They contribute to wrongly condemning yourself for the simple, human act of feeling.

Moreover, many people feel a sense of embarrassment when they have to physically act out emotions to express how they feel outwardly. Learning to shed expectation and judgments in this regard will make it easier for you to embrace emotional expression and release in a meaningful way. With that said, it's important to avoid labeling your body or associated concepts as "good" or "bad."

Flowing and Expressive Movement Practices

Flowing and expressive movement are powerful tools for releasing, connecting, and expressing emotions. It involves smooth and connected motions that in turn make your mind-body connection feel smoother and includes many types of techniques:

- **Freeform dance**: You can engage with freeform dancing to help connect with your emotions. In order to do so, you should
    - play music that resonates with your emotions or sets the mood
    - begin moving freely, allowing your body to respond to the music without any set choreography
    - focus on the sensations in your body and let your movements express your current emotional state
    - explore a range of speeds, levels, and dynamics in your dance.

- **Body mapping**: This tool will help you focus on areas where you feel tension or need to release it. In order to do so, stand with your feet shoulder-length apart and in a comfortable position. Close your eyes and let your attention shift to different parts of the body, intuitively moving in response to your emotions.
- **Emotional flow sequence**: Design a sequence of movements that represent different emotions. Then, connect the emotions through flowing and expressive movements. Go through the sequence, allowing yourself to fully embody each emotion as you move through the corresponding motions.
- **Breath and movement integration**: Because somatic therapy emphasizes the connections between techniques and elements of being, it's a good idea to tie breathing and movement together. You can sync your movements with your breath by inhaling as you expand and open your body and exhaling as you contract and release. You can also use different breathing methods specifically.
- **Props and imagery**: You can enhance your flow and movement through using props like scarves and ribbons or including imagery that tells a story.

As you work with flow and movement, it's important that you create a safe space for yourself. You can start doing so by removing judgmental attitudes and facets from your space, both when it comes to your own ideas and the expectations of others. This highlights the importance of private space within your practice—even if it means working with your movement flows in the shower (safely, of course).

After the movement session, take a few moments for gentle reflection or journaling to process any emotions that surfaced. Remember, these practices are about self-discovery and emotional release. Listen to your body, and feel free to adapt or modify the movements to suit your comfort level.

Dance as a Form of Emotional Expression

In addition to impromptu movement and breathing, you can work with dance as a form of expression and release for somatic therapy. Dance is a powerful and therapeutic form of emotional expression that allows you to connect with their feelings, release pent-up emotions, and foster a sense of well-being. It is accompanied by myriad therapeutic benefits:

- **Embodied expression**: Dance allows you to have a tangible and physical outlet through which you can express your emotions, helping you embody and show your feelings through movement.
- **Stress reduction**: Dancing and other exercise naturally promotes the release of endorphins, which can foster positive mood boosts and lower stress.
- **Mind-body connection**: Dance also naturally heightens the mind-body connection, allowing you to be more aware of your physical sensations and emotional states.

- **Creative outlet**: In addition, dance allows you to uniquely express yourself in a non-verbal manner. This can give you the opportunity to express complex emotions that may evade you verbally.
- **Increased energy and vitality**: Moving the body through dance can enhance energy levels and promote a sense of vitality, contributing to overall emotional well-being.

You also have countless options for somatic therapy-related movement outside of freeform movement. For instance, you can work with emotion-inspired dance by picking an emotion you want to explore, setting relevant music up, and then trying to express that emotion through dance. Here are some other options:

- **Guided imagery dance**: Let a story unfold in your mind thanks to a guided imagery audio. As it does, dance and use movements to visually represent the story. This helps you understand how movement can represent emotions and actions.
- **Body scan dance**: Combining a body scan with dance can help you bring awareness to different parts of the body while simultaneously alleviating tension and expressing emotions.
- **Partner dance**: With a partner, you can take turns leading, following, and going back and forth with different ideas and concepts to intertwine dance and communication.

You're also not confined solely to these ideas. Dancing is an art form, which means that you can personalize it freely to fit your needs.

Guided Imagery for Physical and Emotional Release

The last main concept of release that I have to share with you is the use of guided imagery to release physical and emotional buildup. When you work with guided imagery, the mind is able to find peace that relaxes and reflects through the body. Let's talk about why guided imagery is unparalleled for the mind-body connection and all manner of releases.

The Power of Guided Imagery

Guided imagery is powerful and versatile. It helps you tap into the mind-body connection while guiding you to the path of releasing physical and emotional tension. It involves using the imagination to create vivid mental images, engaging the senses, and influencing the somatic experience. The following represents the various powers of guided imagery, letting you know just what you can hope to achieve thanks to guided imagery:

- **Accessing and releasing tension**: Guided imagery can help you enter a deep state of relaxation. It creates a mental space that empowers you to explore and release tension through the visualization of calming scenes. It promotes the reduction of stress hormones and a sense of ease.

- **Mind-body connection**: The mind and body are intricately connected, and guided imagery serves as a bridge between the two. Imagining specific scenarios or environments can evoke physiological responses, influencing heart rate, breathing, and muscle tension. This means that you can positively impact your well-being with guided imagery.
- **Impact on somatic experiences**: Guided imagery can improve somatic experiences like your perception of sensations and emotions, thus helping you enhance and further your growth and well-being.
- **Versatility**: Guided imagery is adaptable and can be tailored to individuals at different stages of their somatic journey. For those just starting, simple and calming visualizations can be used to introduce the concept of mental imagery and relaxation. Someone further along can dive into specific, targeted practices as well.
- **Integration**: Guided imagery can be seamlessly integrated with other somatic practices, such as breathwork, meditation, or body-focused techniques. Combining guided imagery with movement, like dance or yoga, enhances the mind-body connection and provides a holistic approach to releasing tension.

Taking the time to hone your guided imagery skills can truly improve your ability to work with somatic release and growth.

Creating Imaginative Release Scenarios

A common tactic for guided imagery that helps with somatic therapy release is a personalized release imagery scenario. This will help you engage with your senses and experiences through emotionally resonant mental images. You can work with this method by following these steps:

1. **Setting the stage**: Find a quiet and comfortable space where you can relax, either sitting or lying down. Close your eyes if you're comfortable—which will help you engage with the imaginative process—or simply let your gaze rest softly in the distance.
2. **Grounding and relaxation**: Before you begin, work with a grounding exercise to help you tune in to the relaxed state necessary to connect with guided imagery. You can use the breathing exercises or PMR mentioned earlier to help you achieve a grounded state.
3. **Choose a relaxing environment**: Think about a relaxing environment that brings you a profound sense of peace and relaxation. This could be a serene beach, a lush forest, a quiet meadow, or any other location that resonates with you.
4. **Engage your senses**: Now that you've identified your environment, it's time to engage your senses as you analyze the environment. Take the mind's eye to what you can see, hear, smell, touch, and even taste within this relaxing setting. Really embrace the setting as if you were there through your senses.

5. **Emotional connection**: You should then connect with the emotional experiences of this imagery-based space, asking yourself questions like
    a. What emotions are present in this serene environment?
    b. Are there any emotions that need acknowledgment or release?
    c. How does the environment reflect your emotional state?
6. **Symbolic elements**: Take a look into symbolic elements that can help with release. This could be visualized as a gentle breeze carrying away stress, a stream washing away negativity, or a radiant light dispersing tension. You can make up your own symbols or research ones that you'd like to include in your imagery.
7. **Include physical movement**: Because physical movement can be helpful when it comes to release, you can feel free to engage with gentle movements in real life, or you can envision yourself stretching, dancing, or moving in a way that feels liberating and releasing during your imagery.
8. **Positive affirmations**: Integrate positive affirmations or mantras into the guided imagery. These affirmations can be related to relaxation, letting go, and embracing a sense of peace.
9. **Gradual release**: Use imagery to envision the body releasing tension by dissipating or being absorbed by the environment.
10. **Closing**: When you're ready, slowly bring your attention back to the present moment, noticing the

real environment around you. Allow a moment for reflection on any insights or feelings that emerged during the guided imagery.

You can enhance your visualization by considering vivid and detailed mental images, emphasizing colors, textures, and sensations. It's important to use your imagination to the fullest extent so that it evolves based on your personal and emotional needs.

Integration of Guided Imagery With Movement

Combining guided imagery with intentional movement creates a powerful synergy that enhances the mind-body connection, providing a holistic release experience. By combining vivid mental imagery with purposeful physical movements, you can tap into the world of exploration and catharsis.

In order to work with guided imagery and movement, you should ground and relax to form a connection. Then, you can introduce the visualization-based elements of your environment as mentioned in the previous section. During the process, you can work with movement that helps you explore the environment—like walking, stretching, or dancing.

Let your emotions connect with expressive movements that indicate your personal emotional states as you consider visualized experiences. Integrate imagery that specifically guides the release of physical tension. For example, if imagining a beach, you might visualize tension being washed away with the waves, encouraging corresponding body movements. Flowing transitions and synchronized breathing can be helpful as well.

There are also certain stretches, movements, and exercises that specifically correlate with or are based on guided imagery:

- **Tree stretching**: Imagining yourself as a tree rooted firmly in the ground; you can stretch your arms upward, swaying gently like branches in the wind.
- **Ocean waves flow**: Visualizing the rhythmic flow of ocean waves can translate this imagery into fluid arm movements and gentle swaying of the body.
- **Mountain pose**: Incorporating the imagery of a majestic mountain can help you adopt a strong and grounded mountain pose, emphasizing stability and resilience.
- **Embrace and release**: Guiding yourself to visualize embracing and holding onto tension, followed by a dynamic release movement, such as a sudden exhale and expressive arm movement can benefit you as well.
- **Dance of liberation**: Engage in a spontaneous dance that reflects the emotions and imagery experienced during the guided session.

With these techniques, you have everything you need to work toward releasing the stored tension you face due to trauma or negative emotions and past events. But your journey isn't over just because you've released something. In the next chapter, you will uncover how to integrate your experience so that the benefits truly stick.

CHAPTER 6: SOMATIC EXERCISES-PART 3: INTEGRATION

Feelings are much like waves, we can't stop them from coming but we can choose which ones to surf.

—Jonatan Martensson

Integration is the third part or step involved in self-guided somatic therapy. Many people opt to skip the integration phase only to later wonder why it feels like their efforts were in vain. The answer is simple—without integration, none of the efforts of a therapeutic practice stick. Integration revolves around ensuring that your practices impact daily life, thus securing the success of your progress. In this chapter, we will unveil exactly what it takes to integrate your somatic therapy efforts.

Exercises for Integrating Mind-Body Awareness

Much like exercise can help with awareness and release, it also has an immense power to help with mind-body awareness. Through daily practices and skillful use of breathing and sensory awareness, you can harness mind-body awareness that promotes a continued healing journey and encourages daily self-awareness.

Mindful Daily Activities

In order to integrate the experiences of your somatic therapy progress, it's important to find the time for mindful daily activities. Infusing mindfulness into daily activities is a powerful way to cultivate continuous mind-body connection, promoting a sense of presence and awareness in the midst of routine tasks. There are many types of daily mindfulness activities:

- **Walking**: Walking is something that you already do on a daily basis, which means that using the time you spend walking for mindfulness is like killing two birds with one stone. You can infuse walking with mindfulness by paying attention to each step as you walk, feeling the connection between your feet and the ground. Focus on the sensations and movements of your body; if your mind wanders, gently guide it back.
- **Eating**: Eating mindfully encourages you to slow down, which benefits you mentally and physically due to associated digestive benefits. As you eat, engage your senses. Observe the colors, textures, and smells of your food. Take small bites and savor the flavors. Chew slowly and be fully present with each mouthful. Notice the sensations of hunger and fullness and listen to your body's cues.

- **Breathing during commute**: Whether you're driving, walking, or using public transport, use the time to focus on your breath. Take slow, deep breaths, and observe the rise and fall of your chest or the sensation of the breath entering and leaving your nostrils. It can be helpful to use traffic signals as a cue to check in with breathing.
- **Hygiene**: Mindfulness can even be combined with hygiene. During activities like showering or brushing your teeth, bring your attention to the sensory experience. Feel the water on your skin or the bristles on your teeth. Be fully present with the sensations rather than letting your mind wander.
- **Listening**: Mindful listening is wonderful for improving your connections with others and integrating your experiences. Plus, mindful listening is easy! When engaging in conversations, practice mindful listening. Give your full attention to the speaker, without formulating responses in your mind. Notice the tone, cadence, and emotions conveyed through their words.
- **Breaks**: Whether at work, school, or during a hobby, it's a good idea to take regular breaks to allow you some time to engage with mindfulness. You can work with breathing, stretching, or other simple mindfulness techniques as you do so.
- **Waiting**: So many people view waiting as an inconvenience. Instead, embrace it for the opportunity that it provides to you! You can use otherwise annoying periods of waiting as time to

check in with yourself mindfully—de-stressing you and making time pass by faster in the process. Take a few deep breaths, observe your surroundings, or simply be present with your thoughts and feelings.

- **Cleaning**: Approach household chores with mindfulness. Feel the textures of surfaces, notice the smells of cleaning products, and be fully engaged in the task at hand. Turn cleaning into a meditative practice by focusing on each movement and breath.

And that's just scraping the surface of how you can turn mindfulness into an inherent, daily activity for your success and peace with somatic therapy.

When you embark upon infusing your daily life with mindfulness, it's a good idea to start slow. Rather than going all out with 15 daily mindfulness activities, for instance, pick one or two and start there. Use reminders, such as setting alarms or linking mindfulness practices to specific cues in your environment. Moreover, it's important to approach these activities with a non-judgmental attitude, allowing yourself to be fully present without self-criticism.

Sensory Awareness Practices

Sensory awareness practices are powerful tools for deepening mind-body integration and fostering a holistic somatic experience. These exercises engage the senses—touch, taste, smell, sight, and sound—to bring heightened awareness to the present moment. Let's consider some sensory awareness practices that encourage you to work with each of the five senses mindfully.

First, we have touch. Touch as a sense involves not just texture and pressure, but temperature and other tactile stimulation as well. You can mindfully engage with touch by touching objects with various textures. Close your eyes and explore the textures through touch. Notice the sensations at your fingertips and how they differ. During routine activities like washing your hands or applying lotion, bring full awareness to the tactile sensations. Feel the temperature, texture, and pressure of the water or product against your skin.

Being mindful with taste is as simple as bringing mindfulness into your meals or consumption practices. For example, you can engage with mindful eating as described earlier. You can also engage mindfully with a flavorful drink, like tea, to create an all new habit, using the five senses to engage mindfully before focusing your attention on flavors. This is wonderfully helpful, as many people overlook taste-related sensations and their value daily.

Then, you have the option of engaging with scent or olfactory experiences mindfully, which can be delightful and easy. A common and popular outlet for this is through aromatherapy, involving essential oils, incense, or something similar; however, engaging mindfully with scent is also as simple as taking a walk in nature and being mindful of the different olfactory inputs of nature, like the smell of rain or a flower.

Sight is one of the most common senses used to engage with mindfulness, which means that it can feel repetitive to engage with sight in particular. Despite this, you can spice up your visual mindfulness with tactics that focus on uniquely visual experiences. For example, you can use your favorite piece of art for a color-based meditation. Focus on one color in the piece of art, observing its presence and quality. Take note of any emotions or biased thoughts that arise so you can examine them later.

Finally, there is the sense of hearing. You can easily explore sound by listening to a meditation or playing a musical instrument, listening to the nuances and vibrations of the sound. We often ignore sensory inputs like audio because it can be easy to tune out or listen to as background noise, but it's a good idea to pay special attention to what you hear during mindfulness.

In addition to targeting each sense individually, you also have the option of interacting with sensory systems holistically. For example, you can work with the following practices:

- **Five senses check-in**: Throughout the day, pause and conduct a brief check-in with each sense. Ask yourself what you can see, hear, smell, taste, and touch in the present moment.
- **Sensory walk**: Take a mindful walk where you intentionally focus on each sense. Notice the ground beneath your feet, the sounds of your surroundings, and the feeling of the air against your skin.

- **Mindful shower or bath**: During your shower or bath, be fully present with the sensations. Feel the water on your skin, notice the temperature, and engage with the scents of soap or shampoo.
- **Sensory journaling**: Keep a sensory journal where you document experiences related to each sense. Reflect on how these experiences impact your overall well-being.

So what do these practices have to do with somatic therapy? In one way or another, every single sensory awareness practice that you engage with brings you one step closer to understanding the realities of the world around you. A triggering texture or scent can, with mindfulness, be recognized as just a regular, neutral scent, thus improving your healing trajectory. Moreover, sensory awareness takes present-moment awareness, something crucial to somatic therapy and trauma recovery, and makes it a habit.

Breath-Body Synchronization

The last mindfulness-centered technique that I have for amplifying your integration process is breath-body synchronization. Breath-body synchronization is a practice that emphasizes the harmonious integration of breath with bodily movements, fostering a deep sense of awareness and unity between the mind and body. This intentional pairing of breath and movement can be incorporated into various dynamic activities, promoting grounding and centering throughout daily life.

There are several practices that you can use for breath-body synchronization that are already aligned with mindfulness as a concept. For instance, you can engage in a mindful yoga practice where each movement is synchronized with the breath. Coordinate inhales and exhales with transitions between poses, fostering a sense of flow and presence. Tai Chi is another option you can use to coordinate your breathing with gentle movements.

You don't have to work with mindfulness-specific practices, though. You can tie mindfulness to ordinary exercise practices that you already engage with or want to work with in the future. Cardiovascular exercises and strength training are just two examples of exercises that you can combine with mindfulness and breathing. You can pattern your breathing based on phases or repetitions of a specific exercise, for example.

Additionally, you can make conscious breathing a habit as you carry out daily or mundane tasks. You likely engage with more than a couple of hygiene practices a day—like brushing your teeth or hair, washing your hands, and so on. Using those mundane tasks as an opportunity to stop and work with measured breathing can make mindfulness effortlessly slip into your daily routine. You can also use household chores as a chance to mindfully work on your breathing. For instance, inhale as you lift or reach, and exhale during the release or lowering phase. This approach transforms mundane tasks into opportunities for mindfulness.

Grounding and centering practice, both in and outside of the context of your somatic therapy preparation, can also be points for mindful breathing. You can take five minute breaks throughout the day, for instance, that you use for grounding and centering practices. This can be especially effective if you're overwhelmed or stressed. A great time to implement such a practice is between activities, using transition periods for grounding and centering through breathing.

By weaving breath-body synchronization into dynamic activities and daily tasks, you cultivate a heightened state of awareness, promoting unity between the mind and body. This practice enhances mindfulness, reduces stress, and fosters a sense of grounded presence in each moment of your daily life.

Developing a Daily Somatic Practice

Somatic therapy isn't something that you practice once—or even for a week—and then never touch again. That would be like a recovered addict using their substance of choice after a week sober. Not only would they be discouraged that results didn't stick, but they would have to begin the process over again. Likewise, you should practice somatic therapy regularly for the best benefits. The good news is that somatic therapy doesn't have to take hours out of your day to be a regularity.

Establishing a Consistent Routine

One strategy that you can use for making somatic therapy a regular practice is by establishing a consistent routine that is sustainable and exciting for you to engage with. Beyond simply encouraging continued progress, there is a significant benefit to being consistent in your routines. The brain adapts to repetitive activities, and consistent somatic practices can promote positive changes in neural pathways associated with relaxation and awareness. Furthermore, the body reacts to regular stimuli, which means that consistent efforts will enhance your ability to feel and stay relaxed.

Establishing a consistent routine is as simple as personalizing your daily schedule to involve a new habit. This means that you should make it a point to allocate time slots for somatic exercises. Treat these slots with the same importance as other commitments, recognizing their role in promoting overall well-being. It is also smart to pick a time of day for your practices, like morning or evening. Establishing a connection with a specific part of your day helps create a habit.

It's also helpful if you create a space for your practice that is consistent and dedicated. This could be a corner of a room, a yoga mat, or a specific chair. If you have the ability to use a designated room, then feel free; however, it can be as simple as designating an object to be your space. Customize your practice space with elements that promote relaxation, such as soft lighting, calming colors, or soothing sounds. Make it a space where you feel at ease.

In addition, begin with smaller and more gradual daily sessions rather than diving into regular hours-long ones. You won't feel as pressured or stressed if you begin with smaller sessions. As you become more accustomed to the practices, gradually increase the duration or complexity. Building up slowly helps avoid burnout and reinforces the habit. This means that a five minute journaling session or yoga flow constitutes a perfectly valid, entry-level somatic therapy daily routine.

Making the habit of daily somatic practices truly stick can be done through something called habit stacking. You engage with habit stacks daily. Think about it—do you have a routine when you wake up of any sort? That's a habit stack, even if it's just washing your hands after using the restroom. Similarly, somatic therapy can be turned into a habit stack if you combine associated, pre-existing habits. This makes it easier for the brain to fall into the pattern you aim to create.

Lastly, it's important to track your progress as you go, allowing you to modify your methods and goals for better outcomes. Be sure to be flexible yet consistent, working with various tactics and strategies to help you determine what works best for you.

Short and Accessible Practices

Short and accessible practices are another way that you can make somatic therapy a daily habit that sticks and simultaneously benefits you. Your practices don't have to be long, drawn out, or complicated as you might be led to assume. Short and accessible somatic exercises are designed to be easily integrated into busy schedules, making them ideal for daily practice. This also means that you can create and customize your own practices to fit your needs.

Outside of customizing practices yourself, you have a few different exercises you can take for yourself, including

- 3-minute mindful breathing
    - Sit or stand comfortably.
    - Inhale deeply through your nose for a count of 3.
    - Exhale slowly through your mouth for a count of 3.
    - Repeat for 3 minutes, focusing solely on your breath.
- Seated body scan
    - Sit comfortably with both feet on the ground.
    - Close your eyes and bring attention to your toes.
    - Gradually scan up through your body, noticing sensations in each area.
    - Take 3–5 minutes to complete the scan, releasing tension as you go.
- Desk shoulder release
    - Sit upright at your desk.
    - Inhale as you lift your shoulders toward your ears.
    - Exhale and let your shoulders relax down.
    - Repeat for 1–2 minutes, releasing tension in your shoulders and neck.
- Breath-body awareness walk
    - Take a short walk outdoors.
    - Coordinate your steps with your breath (e.g., inhale for 3 steps, exhale for 3 steps).

    - Focus on the sensation of each step and your breath.
    - Engage for 5–10 minutes, integrating movement and breath.
- 2-minute body shake
    - Stand with feet shoulder-width apart.
    - Shake your body starting from your hands, working down to your feet.
    - Let your body shake freely for 2 minutes, releasing tension and promoting energy flow.
- Mindful stretching break
    - Stand or sit comfortably.
    - Inhale as you reach your arms overhead.
    - Exhale as you gently lean to one side, stretching your side body.
    - Repeat on the other side.
    - Take 3–4 minutes for a quick and mindful stretching break.
- Grounding breath pause
    - Sit comfortably and close your eyes.
    - Inhale deeply through your nose for a count of 4.
    - Hold your breath for a count of 4.
    - Exhale slowly through your mouth for a count of 4.
    - Pause for a moment before repeating for 3–5 minutes.
- Hand awareness meditation
    - Sit comfortably and rest your hands on your lap.

    - Bring your attention to the sensations in your hands.
    - Feel the warmth, tingling, or any other sensations.
    - Stay focused for 2–3 minutes, bringing awareness to your hands.
- Somatic self-massage
    - Choose a body part (e.g., hands, neck, or feet).
    - Massage the area using gentle, circular motions.
    - Focus on the sensations and any areas of tension.
    - Allocate 3–5 minutes for a quick self-massage break.
- Breath-centric mindful pause
    - Pause whatever you're doing.
    - Close your eyes and take 3 deep breaths.
    - Focus solely on the sensations of each breath.
    - This quick pause can be done in 1–2 minutes.

Journaling and Reflection

Journaling is a third amazing option for turning somatic therapy into a daily practice. It can help enhance your self-awareness and deepen your somatic experience through insight, progress tracking, and more. What follows are some journaling prompts that you can use to inform your journaling sessions:

- **Before your somatic practice**
  - How do you feel physically and emotionally right now?
  - Are there specific areas of tension or discomfort that you're aware of?
  - What are your intentions for today's somatic practice?
- **During your somatic practice**
  - Describe any sensations you're experiencing in your body.
  - Are there moments of ease or discomfort?
  - How is your breath during the practice?
  - What emotions, if any, are arising?
- **After your somatic practice**
  - Reflect on any changes in your physical or emotional state.
  - Did you notice any shifts in tension or relaxation?
  - How would you describe your overall sense of well-being after the practice?
- **Tracking progress**
  - What aspects of your somatic practice do you find most beneficial?
  - Have you noticed any patterns or changes over time in your mind-body connection?
  - Are there specific exercises or techniques that resonate with you more than others?
- **Insights and discoveries**
  - Have you gained any new insights about your body or emotions through somatic practices?

  - Are there recurring themes or emotions that come up during your reflective sessions?
  - What have you learned about your body's responses to stress or relaxation?
- **Mind-body integration**
  - Reflect on moments where you felt a strong mind-body connection.
  - How do you carry the benefits of somatic practices into other aspects of your day?
  - Have you noticed increased awareness of your body in everyday activities?
- **Challenges and obstacles**
  - Explore any challenges or obstacles you encountered during your somatic practice.
  - How did you navigate or overcome these challenges?
  - Are there recurring barriers to consistency, and how might you address them?
- **Gratitude and acknowledgment**
  - Express gratitude for the time and effort you dedicated to your somatic practice.
  - Acknowledge any positive changes or moments of growth you've experienced.
  - Celebrate small victories in your journey toward mind-body integration.
- **Integration into daily life**
  - Reflect on how somatic practices influence your daily activities and interactions.

    - In what ways have you incorporated mindfulness into your routine outside of dedicated somatic sessions?
    - Have you noticed any positive impacts on your overall well-being?
- **Future intentions**
    - Set intentions for future somatic practices.
    - What areas of your mind and body would you like to focus on in the upcoming sessions?
    - How can you continue to cultivate a mindful and integrated approach to your daily life?

Furthermore, you can take into consideration some tips for journaling that will improve the overall experience. For example, it's important to be open and honest with your journaling experience so that you can understand your somatic experiences and how you work with them. Journal regularly, even if it's only a sentence or two, to track your journey—and be sure to review those entries regularly. Moreover, don't feel confined to just pen and paper or even to written journaling; you can draw, record yourself, make a collage, and more.

Overall, somatic therapy is something that you should work with, even a little, on a daily basis. Daily efforts contribute to steady and assured integration of somatic therapy experiences, leading to a far happier life and more fruitful efforts.

Long-Term Strategies for Embodied Wellness

Integrating somatic experiences also has to do with the long-term, which involves long-term strategies that contribute to holistic and sustained wellness. Specifically, this means that you have to let the benefits of somatic therapy extend to your overall life, and you should also diversify your methods and increase their intensity over time.

Progression and Gradual Expansion

Over time, your somatic therapy methods and practices will need to expand. It's a simple fact, and the recognition of it will lead to a more mindful approach to your personal growth journey. Beyond that, allowing your practices to progress will do wonders for ensuring that you can continue to grow, assess new experiences, and otherwise improve to have a more fulfilling, trauma-reduced life.

In order to allow your practices to progress over time, it's important to begin with the fundamental practices that I've provided to you thus far. All of these foundational practices—like breath awareness, gentle movements, and body scanning—contribute to an enhanced ability to move forward with grace. Then, you also need to make consistency key as you progress so that your efforts build upon one another for maximum benefits.

Progression and gradual expansion also rely on listening to your body. Pay close attention to how your body responds to different somatic exercises. Listen to sensations, comfort levels, and any signals your body may provide. This can help you know what's working and what isn't, as well as what you need to spend more or less time focusing on. If certain exercises feel challenging or uncomfortable, consider modifying them or exploring alternative approaches. Gradually introduce new elements as your body becomes more accustomed.

As you continue your practice, you will need to progressively raise the intensity and duration of your practices to intensify and widen the range of effects. This could involve deeper stretches, longer sessions, or more intricate movements. Increase the duration of your somatic practices gradually. You can do this by tacking on a few minutes extra at the end of your sessions, allowing your mind and body to adapt with each progression.

You should also make an effort to diversify what techniques you use, exploring different modalities and elements within your practice. Naturally, it's fine to have a favorite modality and stick to it, but trying other elements can empower your practice and help you achieve more benefits. Because of this, I definitely recommend using elements mentioned in this book as a checklist. If you have the ability to try something out, I would try to do everything in this book with regard to your somatic experiences at least once.

Progressing your somatic therapy experiences also involves setting mindful intentions. Before a session, it's important to set an intention and then reflect on that intention after the fact. Are you seeking stress relief, increased awareness, or specific physical benefits? Align your practices with these intentions. You should also set intentions for progression, whether it's a fitness or self-discovery related goal.

To ensure that you're still on track, periodic self-assessments can be a big help. Use reflective practices, such as journaling, to document insights, challenges, and moments of growth. Acknowledge and celebrate milestones in your somatic journey. Whether it's mastering a new movement or achieving a deeper state of relaxation, recognize your achievements.

Progression also involves making somatic self-therapy a lifelong journey. It might seem discouraging at first to know that, in a sense, you will never be fully healed; however, embracing your healing journey as a long-term process will be more rewarding. Everyone spends their life healing from something—whether it be a bad relationship, childhood trauma, or self-hatred—and by embracing your unique journey, you will find more growth, love, and success.

Diversification of Somatic Techniques

Earlier, I mentioned the value that can be found in diversifying your methods for somatic therapy. It might seem challenging just to do this, though. There are a few tips that can make the process of diversifying your somatic techniques far easier:

- **Explore different modalities**: Make it a point to try different modalities like movement, breathing, meditation, and expressive art methods. By working with different methods, you can find what works and experience a wider range of benefits.
- **Attend classes and workshops**: Classes and workshops are offered that pertain to somatic practices, which can teach you a lot about unique techniques and perspectives. Sometimes, such classes offer guest instructors that can provide you with access to more professional-grade techniques without professional rates.
- **Online resources and apps**: Resources like websites, apps, and virtual classes can be wonderful for connecting with others, learning from experiences of others, and finding new techniques that benefit your practice.
- **Rotate exercises**: Regularly make space for rotating and including diverse exercises into your routine. For example, alternate between yoga, mindful walking, and breath-focused sessions throughout the week. Be sure to integrate new exercises mindfully by paying attention to how your body and mind respond to them.
- **Adjust seasonally**: Some exercises, like nature walks, are more suited to spring and summer months, whereas indoor exercises can be beneficial in autumn and winter. Seasons also encourage natural connection during different parts of the year.

Even if you don't feel like engaging with somatic therapy on a particular day, it's important to remember that the process of integration is an ongoing effort. Missing integrative periods can jeopardize the long-term success of your somatic therapy, so remember that it's important to integrate.

CHAPTER 7:
COMBINING SOMATIC THERAPY WITH OTHER MODALITIES

Healing is a matter of time, but it is sometimes also a matter of opportunity.

—Hippocrates

How Somatic Therapy Complements Other Therapeutic Practices

When it comes to considering therapeutic methods that empower your healing journey, it is important to consider other methods as well. By this, I mean that you should consider other methods of therapy that go alongside somatic therapy, resulting in more holistic and empowering benefits in the process. Let's think about how somatic therapy complements other therapeutic practices.

Understanding Therapeutic Synergy

When it comes to considering somatic therapy alongside other methods, an important concept to understand is that of therapeutic synergy. Therapeutic synergy refers to the combined and enhanced effects of integrating different therapeutic modalities to address various aspects of an individual's well-being. In the context of somatic therapy, which focuses on the mind-body connection and physical sensations, there are several ways in which it can synergize with other therapeutic approaches.

For example, let's take holistic healing. Somatic therapy contributes to holistic healing by recognizing the interconnectedness of the mind and body. When combined with other therapeutic modalities such as talk therapy or cognitive-behavioral approaches, it allows for a comprehensive understanding and treatment of your mental, emotional, and physical well-being.

The emotional release that often coincides with somatic therapy is something else that can interlink with other forms of therapy. Somatic therapy often works with exploring and releasing emotions that are stored throughout the body. When combined with traditional psychotherapy, it can facilitate a deeper emotional release, as verbal expression is complemented by the physical processing of emotions. Moreover, somatic therapy is particularly effective in addressing trauma stored in the body. Integrating it with trauma-focused therapies like eye movement desensitization and reprocessing therapy, also known as EMDR, can provide a more thorough approach to trauma healing.

Then, it is important to think about how somatic therapy focuses on the mind-body connection and self-awareness. When combined with mindfulness practices, yoga, or meditation, it enhances awareness and promotes self-regulation, contributing to overall mental and physical well-being. Beyond that, integrating somatic therapy with psychodynamic therapy or existential therapy can deepen self-reflection and insight, fostering personal growth and development.

All methods also have the benefit of adding stress reduction through varied practices and structures. When combined with cognitive-behavioral strategies or relaxation techniques, for example, somatic therapy offers a more comprehensive approach to stress reduction.

The point in saying this isn't to undermine the individual power or integrity of somatic therapy; rather, it is to highlight that there is power when we consider the unique contributions of individual methods and how those contributions can stack to form uniquely empowered benefits.

Collaborative Therapeutic Integration

Somatic therapy is often used in conjunction with something called collaborative therapeutic integration, which involves bringing together practitioners from different therapeutic modalities to create a cohesive and comprehensive treatment plan for individuals. Understanding the key components of this concept is vital to understanding the potential of somatic therapy to work well with other modalities.

One of the main concepts that you should know for combining somatic therapy with other modalities is self-directed learning. Self-directed learning involves taking learning about somatic therapy principles and techniques into your own hands. Online courses, books, and resources can provide a foundation for understanding the mind-body connection. Moreover, personal experiences can direct your learning as you pick up tips and tricks from others.

Then, you also have the option of integrating somatic therapy alongside an existing therapeutic approach. If you already attend therapy or work with self-guided methods for healing, then you can add somatic therapy into the mix either by asking your therapist or working toward it on your own. Take the time to examine where somatic practices could enhance your overall practice and contribute to a more holistic understanding of well-being.

Furthermore, it is wise to consider networking and related options for connecting with others who engage with somatic therapy as a practice. Connect with peers or online communities to exchange insights and experiences. Also, make it a point to participate in discussions or forums where practitioners from different modalities share how they integrate somatic elements into their self-guided practices.

I also recommend exploring multi-disciplinary resources as you learn more about somatic therapy. Multi-disciplinary resources serve as guidance for those who work in intersecting fields; therefore, referencing them can be particularly helpful when it comes to studying self-guided somatic therapy in correlation with other modalities. You can learn how those modalities work together and how their idiosyncrasies can be helpful for your own practice.

Another strategy for understanding the benefit of self-guided collaborative therapeutic integration is to reflect on your somatic practices regularly. Take the time to reflect on what is and isn't working within your practice. When you do reflect, you can highlight parts of your practice that you wish were stronger, or you can take a look at where other therapeutic modalities can fill in those blanks.

It's also important that you set goals for your practice and journey. Even if you find that one goal isn't achievable within the scope of somatic therapy, you can look into other modalities and determine whether another modality might be more effective. For instance, somatic therapy might not be able to reframe negative and distorted thoughts, but cognitive behavioral therapy can.

Addressing Mind-Body Connections in Conjunction

When you consider methods in conjunction with one another, it is also important to refresh yourself on the mind-body connection. This will help your efforts be more holistic and informed based on the interplay of mental and physical well-being. You've already come to understand the mind-body connection in the context of somatic therapy, but let's add to that understanding.

Embrace the biopsychosocial model, which considers biological, psychological, and social factors in understanding health and illness. This model underscores the need for an integrated approach to address the complexities of well-being. This can be worked with by considering the dynamic interplay between various therapeutic modalities.

How Somatic Therapy Enhances EMDR

EMDR is another powerful yet underestimated method of healing from trauma. It involves rapid eye movements to help the brain reprocess traumatic memories, and it can be especially helpful when used in conjunction with other modalities—somatic therapy included.

Preparing the Ground With Somatic Techniques

EMDR can be followed or preceded by somatic therapy. Personally, I recommend using somatic therapy as a way to lead into your EMDR therapy sessions. Somatic therapy, which focuses on the mind-body connection, can easily become a powerful tool for creating a safe and grounded space before delving into the profound work of EMDR.

Somatic interventions serve as a bridge between the cognitive and physical aspects of trauma. By incorporating practices that engage the body, you can become more attuned to your sensations, emotions, and bodily responses. This exploration becomes crucial groundwork for the subsequent EMDR sessions. In other words, you can certainly use somatic therapy as a precursor to grounded and stable EMDR sessions, boosting the benefits of both.

One way that you can bridge the gap between these two practices is by working with your breathwork. Both EMDR and somatic therapy use very similar breathwork-related exercises for grounding and preparation. This means that your somatic therapy preparation can double as EMDR preparation easily. Furthermore, the breathing tactics you master from somatic therapy can translate directly to EMDR benefits.

In order to combine EMDR with somatic therapy, there are a few other considerations to keep in mind to make the practice comfortable and safe. For example, you will recall that creating a safe space for somatic therapy was important; the same goes for EMDR. Being as you likely have a space set up for your somatic therapy practice, you can then work on forging a therapeutic alliance with yourself or a professional.

You can, of course, self-guide yourself through the process of somatic therapy. However, if you're working with a professional, it is wise to let them know that you want to fuse the two practices—and what you hope to get out of it. If you're guiding yourself through the experience, set vows and goals for yourself—even forming a contract as you did earlier. Ensuring that you know what to expect and your goals will drive success.

Now, you might be wondering how EMDR and somatic therapy can combine for profound benefits. The collusion is simple:

- Somatic approaches facilitate access to implicit memory, where trauma is often stored. Establishing a foundation through somatic techniques allows for a more gradual and regulated exploration of these memories. This not only minimizes the risk of overwhelming clients but also enhances the efficacy of subsequent EMDR sessions.

- Recognizing that each individual progresses at their own pace is paramount. Somatic techniques provide a nuanced approach, respecting the readiness of clients to engage in EMDR. This personalized foundation ensures a more tailored and effective trauma processing experience.

Therefore, combining the two modalities can be excellent for healing from trauma, especially because trauma is a main focus of EMDR. It's like using somatic therapy for the body and EMDR for the mind!

Enhancing EMDR Processing With Somatic Integration

Integration goes beyond what we talked about in Chapter 6; you can also use integration to integrate somatic therapy into the framework of EMDR. In other words, you can improve your work with EMDR by adding touches of or supports from somatic therapy. This powerful tag team can make it far easier for you to process or reprocess trauma, benefiting your mind, body, and soul.

By integrating somatic techniques directly into EMDR sessions, you can adopt a holistic approach to trauma healing, even in your self-guided practices. EMDR traditionally focuses on bilateral stimulation—which involves working both sides of the brain—to process distressing memories, almost like dislodging them when they've gotten stuck. But the inclusion of somatic elements broadens the therapeutic landscape. This combination allows for a more comprehensive exploration of the mind-body connection during trauma processing.

Because of this, somatic techniques can be invaluable in the scope of an EMDR session. Establishing a foundation of safety and connection through somatic interventions before diving into memory reprocessing enhances your overall resilience to the methods, making the reprocessing of that trauma easier to bear. This approach ensures that you are better equipped to navigate the emotional terrain that EMDR may unearth.

Body-informed bilateral stimulation is just one way that you can combine somatic therapy within the scope of EMDR. It enhances the effectiveness of traditional EMDR protocols by combining a mind-body connection-privy approach alongside one that uses bodily awareness for healing. This embodied approach creates a more immersive and interconnected therapeutic environment.

In addition, one can combine somatic therapy and EMDR through movement and expressive art forms. By using somatic body-based release strategies like meditation and dance inside of the framework of EMDR therapy, you can more readily embody your personal narrative. As you know, movement is powerful for releasing stored trauma, which can provide an alternative outlet for EMDR therapy than what is traditionally recommended. Integrating expressive arts fosters creativity and self-expression, complementing the cognitive processing inherent in EMDR.

Somatic therapy is also particularly valuable in the scope of EMDR because it can help bridge relevant gaps when it comes to trauma reprocessing. For example, if you're working to overcome the trauma of an assault, you might not remember all of the details of it. This can be troublesome, as EMDR interventions encourage visualization of the traumatic event. Where this isn't possible, somatic therapy and memories/trauma trapped in the body can come out to play, bridging that gap and improving recovery.

Finally, somatic therapy can improve your emotional regulation during EMDR practices. Usually, EMDR brings out emotions that are hard to manage; however, coupled with the unique expression provided by somatic therapy, these emotions can be easier to manage. As you engage with your bodily sensations, you can guide yourself in regulating emotions that may arise during memory reprocessing.

This dual-focus on cognitive and somatic elements fosters a more balanced and manageable emotional experience. By embracing embodied approaches, you can facilitate a more comprehensive and integrated experience, ultimately enhancing the resolution of traumatic memories and supporting yourself on your path to healing.

Post-EMDR Somatic Integration Practices

Even after an EMDR session is done, you can engage with somatic therapy in combination with your methods. This means that after an EMDR session ends, not only can you integrate with EMDR methods, but you can integrate with somatic therapy methods. For instance, this might look like

1. somatic therapy: grounding and centering for the experience of EMDR
2. EMDR: running through preparatory steps for EMDR therapy
3. somatic therapy/EMDR combo: using both EMDR and somatic therapy during a session
4. EMDR: EMDR-typical integration
5. somatic therapy: final integration through somatic therapy.

There are two particularly excellent somatic integration tools that you can work with after EMDR: body scanning and natural grounding. After you finish a session, it can be beneficial to integrate your experiences through either of these practices. The body scan technique encourages you to reconnect with your bodily sensations in the present moment, promoting a sense of groundedness. Connecting with nature can also provide a tangible and grounding experience alongside the other benefits of time in nature. This connection aids in anchoring you in the present and supporting the integration of EMDR insights.

Outside of mere integration, somatic therapy post-EMDR can also contribute to healing through the sustaining of bodily awareness. Introducing regular practices that enhance body awareness, such as yoga or tai chi, supports the integration of EMDR work into daily life. These practices become tools for resilience, which helps you to navigate challenges with a heightened sense of self-awareness.

As you can see, somatic therapy and EMDR can certainly go hand-in-hand. If you're interested in further reading, feel free to check out my self-guided handbook for EMDR therapy, *EMDR Workbook: Start the Process of Healing From PTSD, Trauma, and Anxiety Today.*

Case Studies: Somatic Therapy in Action

In order to help you understand the efficacy of somatic interventions in real life, I've included sample case studies and examples that show the literal ways somatic therapy can work. All names, sensitive information, and instances of minor details have been altered to hide client privacy, and some individuals take inspiration from real-world accounts.

Illustrating Somatic Interventions

Somatic therapy is helpful in a wide variety of contexts. Up until now, you might have thought that you need to do it all for somatic benefits—combining methods and using every strategy every time for results. That's far from the truth; as you will see, many individuals have been able to power through and heal with just one or two somatic therapy interventions.

Case Study #1: Trauma Resolution Through Breathwork

Sarah, a survivor of a traumatic event, struggled with overwhelming anxiety and hypervigilance. Traditional talk therapy alone proved challenging for her to process the deep-seated trauma. It felt like the work she was doing in cognitive behavioral therapy didn't do anything; she understood it in an abstract sense, but when it came down to it, the strategies didn't work. It felt like something was missing.

After a few sessions with no improvements, Sarah's therapist recommended a somatic intervention powered by breathwork. At first, Sarah didn't expect this to be a powerful method or to even help slightly; however, desperate, she gave it a shot. During this intervention, Sarah learned to engage with her breath, allowing her to regulate her nervous system. This practice became a foundation for further trauma exploration.

Over time, Sarah reported a significant reduction in anxiety levels. The breathwork not only provided immediate relief but also paved the way for more profound trauma processing in subsequent therapy sessions, ultimately leading to resolution and healing.

Case Study #2: Body-Informed Bilateral Stimulation for PTSD

Michael, a military veteran, struggled with severe PTSD symptoms. Traditional EMDR alone was challenging due to his heightened startle response and discomfort with eye movements. As a result, while EMDR seemed to be the best intervention for him, he simply couldn't bear traditional methods. This led him to a therapist who was experienced with body-informed bilateral stimulation as opposed to the traditional eye movements.

The therapist integrated body-informed bilateral stimulation by incorporating gentle tapping on Michael's shoulders. This approach allowed for bilateral stimulation while respecting Michael's somatic sensitivities. As a result, Michael experienced a notable reduction in PTSD symptoms. The body-informed approach provided an alternative pathway for processing traumatic memories, demonstrating the adaptability of somatic interventions to meet individual needs.

Case Study #3: Dance Movement Therapy for Emotional Expression

Maria, dealing with the aftermath of a toxic relationship, found it challenging to express and process her emotions verbally. She struggled with the traditional, more direct methods of therapy that were offered. Eventually, dance movement therapy was introduced as a somatic intervention. Through guided movement, Maria discovered a non-verbal outlet for expressing her emotions and reclaiming a sense of autonomy over her body.

Within just a few sessions, Maria reported a newfound sense of empowerment and emotional release. The integration of dance movement therapy allowed her to connect with her emotions on a deeper level, illustrating the capacity of somatic interventions to tap into non-cognitive forms of healing.

These real-world case studies illuminate the versatility and transformative potential of somatic interventions. Somatic therapy doesn't have to be a strict, textbook experience. It can be combined with various outcomes, personalized, and used to treat varying individuals, regardless of the trauma.

Tailoring Approaches to Individual Needs

The art of somatic therapy lies in its ability to adapt and tailor interventions to meet the unique needs of each client. Let's take a look at three more case studies that demonstrate just how profoundly somatic therapy can be tailored to the individual.

Case Study #4: Adaptive Breathwork for Anxiety Management

James, experiencing debilitating anxiety, struggled with traditional talk therapy methods. His heightened anxiety often hindered the effectiveness of somatic interventions. His somatic therapist recognized James's challenge and adapted breathwork techniques to accommodate his anxiety levels. The pace and intensity of the breathwork were adjusted, ensuring a gradual and manageable progression.

The decision to adapt the breathwork stemmed from a collaborative discussion with James, emphasizing his comfort and agency in the therapeutic process. This client-centered approach allowed for a tailored intervention that aligned with James's unique needs. As a result, James has experienced a significant decline in his anxiety and an improved ability to cope.

Case Study #5: Multi-Modal Somatic Approaches for Expressive Healing

Carlos, struggling with emotional expression, found verbal communication challenging. Traditional therapeutic methods did not fully address his need for expressive outlets. His therapist was able to consider Carlos's unique needs and thus employed a multi-modal approach, integrating somatic techniques such as art therapy, movement, and sound exploration. This allowed Carlos to express himself nonverbally in a way that felt authentic to his experience.

The decision to use a multi-modal approach was guided by an initial assessment of Carlos's preferences and strengths. In other words, Carlos's preferences and needs were taken into consideration rather than applying a one-size-fits-all approach. The therapist aimed to create a therapeutic environment that resonated with Carlos's unique mode of expression, facilitating a more holistic and personalized healing journey.

Case Study #6: Customized Movement Practices for PTSD

Emma is a survivor of complex trauma who faced challenges in traditional EMDR sessions due to triggers associated with specific movements. Her therapist developed customized movement practices that allowed Emma to engage in somatic interventions without triggering distress. This involved collaborative exploration of movements that felt safe and empowering for Emma. Her therapist prioritized creating a sense of agency for Emma, ensuring that somatic interventions aligned with her personal boundaries and comfort levels. As a result, Emma was able to work through traumatic experiences without heightened distress.

While these individuals used the power of professionally guided therapy, their experiences go to show how you can tailor your own experience for effective results. You don't have to follow everything to a T when it is your own personalized healing journey, especially if you're your own therapist.

Clearly, somatic therapy has the unique ability to combine alongside other methods of therapy—particularly modalities that aren't as familiar with body-informed interventions—for more holistic and impressive benefits. Don't feel like you have to give up on your existing treatment just to make room for somatic therapy; undoubtedly, the two can intersect.

CHAPTER 8:
OVERCOMING CHALLENGES AND MOVING FORWARD

Someone once asked me, "Why do you always insist on taking the hard road?" I replied, "Why do you assume I see two roads?"

—Unknown

We're almost at the end of our journey together, which is why this chapter focuses on helping you overcome common challenges associated with somatic therapy and how you can continue making progress throughout the journey—even when it seems like you've hit the roadblock to end all roadblocks.

Addressing Common Challenges in Somatic Practice

Embarking on a self-guided somatic practice can be a transformative journey, yet it often comes with challenges. Rather than leaving you to manage those challenges alone, it is important to head into somatic therapy armed with strategies that can help you overcome conflicts and resistance.

Navigating Resistance and Discomfort

Speaking of resistance, resistance is one of the hallmark challenges of somatic therapy. Somatic therapy inherently involves a lot of practices that can make some people rather uncomfortable. It involves a high level of vulnerability, which can make exposing your body to various forms of expression rather troubling. What's more is that new sensations or movements can be quite unsettling during the experience, and discomfort often arises as a protective response to the unknown or repressed emotions and memories stored in the body. Unearthing these sensations can trigger a sense of vulnerability.

At the same time, this resistance doesn't have to hold you back from making great strides in your progress. Let's review some methods that you can use to overcome resistance:

- **Mindful awareness**: The foundation of navigating resistance lies in cultivating mindful awareness. It is important that you observe your resistance without judgment in order to develop the ability to explore potential resistance from a place of non-reactivity.
- **Gradual progression and patience**: Recognizing that somatic exploration is a gradual process can alleviate resistance. Breaking down the practice into manageable steps and progressing at an individualized pace fosters a sense of safety and control.
- **Journaling and reflection**: Incorporating journaling as a reflective tool can deepen self-awareness. This highlights the value of examining your experiences, thoughts, and emotions through journaling.

Moreover, it is important to hone a mindset that allows you to recognize discomfort as a gateway to healing. Some ways that you can consider discomfort as a gateway to healing include considering the following:

- **Sensation awareness**: Heightened discomfort can signify an increased awareness of bodily sensations. This heightened sensitivity may indicate that you are on the brink of uncovering and releasing stored tension.
- **Emotional release**: Discomfort can be a precursor to emotional release. As you push through resistance, emotions that were once suppressed may surface, offering an opportunity for catharsis and healing.
- **Shifts in posture and energy**: Observing shifts in body posture and energy during somatic practice can indicate the release of held tension. These subtle changes often accompany a transformative shift in the body's response to somatic exploration.

Dealing With Impatience and Frustration

Somatic therapy isn't always going to be a linear or smooth process; it involves navigating challenges, including impatience and frustration. By exploring how you can overcome impatience and frustrations, you gain the ability to push through and succeed despite hurdles. This begins with understanding *why* you feel impatient or frustrated.

Typically, impatience in the face of healing or self-discovery stems from a desire for immediate results or resolutions, which isn't something that any therapeutic modality can provide. The somatic journey involves self-exploration, which is inherently dynamic and may not follow a linear progression. Still, this can be a frustrating experience, and that frustration is in and of itself very telling. Frustration can serve as a signal that one is pushing against personal boundaries or encountering resistance. It may indicate the presence of unexplored emotional or physical territories within the somatic experience.

Fending off your frustrations and impatience might seem like a constant uphill battle, but there are actually numerous tactics that you can use to help you get through those troubling feelings—even while actively engaging with somatic therapy:

- **Mindful breath and centering**: In moments of impatience, turning to mindful breathwork and centering techniques can provide a sense of immediate relief. Focusing on the breath helps ground you in the present moment, easing the tension that you may be feeling and the pressure of needing to progress.
- **Adjusting expectations**: Acknowledging that the somatic journey is a process with its own timeline is crucial. Adjusting expectations and understanding that growth takes time can alleviate frustration and prevent feelings of discouragement.

- **Seeking support and guidance**: Getting support, either in the form of a community or professional guidance, can offer valuable perspectives that foster connection and provide encouragement during challenging moments.

In addition, shifting your perspective to be more growth-aligned and realistic can prevent discouragement and frustration. Try to avoid viewing impatience and frustration as obstacles; instead, consider them to be powerful catalysts and opportunities for self-exploration and growth. Each moment of discomfort becomes a chance to deepen self-awareness and resilience within the somatic journey.

Furthermore, it becomes easier to work through such blockages if you embrace somatic therapy as a learning experience and growth-based practice rather than a means to an end. Embracing the somatic journey as a continuous learning process reframes frustration as a natural aspect of exploration. Each challenge becomes a lesson contributing to personal growth and self-discovery.

Finally, you have to give yourself the grace and ability to celebrate small victories. As you work with somatic therapy, you may not achieve your biggest goals immediately, but you will undoubtedly achieve something to be proud of. Recognizing and celebrating small achievements along the way instills a sense of accomplishment. Breaking down the journey into manageable milestones allows you to appreciate progress and maintain motivation during what will undoubtedly be a lifelong process.

Adapting Practices to Individual Needs

Somatic therapy is a practice that is inherently personal, which means that its effectiveness lies within its ability to be adapted. Tailoring practices to individual preferences, addressing physical limitations, and meeting evolving needs is what makes somatic therapy so useful in the first place. We all have unique preferences, so modifying, combining, and altering somatic practices can lead to their collaborative exploration and profound results.

As you think about somatic therapy practices, it is crucial to understand that what works for one might not work for another; practices I use will differ greatly from the ones you use. For example, think back to the first case study in Chapter 7. Sarah used breathwork to conquer her anxiety, but you might benefit more from grounding and meditation. Both approaches are equally valid and worthy.

This means that you have to consider both your physical and mental limitations, as well as recognize how your practice needs to evolve over time to keep up with your progress. You should feel comfortable embracing change and make dynamic decisions for your practice that evolve with your needs and desires.

Strategies for Maintaining Progress

As you work with somatic therapy, there may be periods where you feel like you're not progressing or even that you've regressed when it comes to your progress. While this can be discouraging, it is also incredibly normal. The adage that progress isn't linear has never been truer than it is here. Still, it can be helpful and motivating to have a toolkit of strategies that help you maintain progress.

Establishing Sustainable Routines

Mentioned earlier, you can integrate somatic practices by working with sustainable routines; however, this is also a necessary strategy when it comes to continuing your progress and overcoming stagnation. Therefore, I wanted to mention some strategies you can use to overcome roadblocks and maintain sustainable routines that contribute to enhanced somatic experiences.

- **Mindful integration**: Integrate mindfulness into your daily routines for a touch of seamless somatic integration. This includes incorporating mindful breathing during routine tasks or bringing awareness to bodily sensations while engaged in daily activities. As mentioned in earlier sections, this can involve simple inclusions like mindful walking, waiting, or eating to stack habits.
- **Ritualize somatic practices**: Creating rituals around somatic practices establishes a sense of routine and importance. This could involve setting aside a specific time each day, creating a dedicated space for practice, or incorporating somatic exercises into existing rituals like morning routines or bedtime rituals. Make sure that your rituals are both simple and attractive, inspiring you to engage with them on a daily basis.

- **Start small and build**: Initiating a sustainable routine involves starting with small, manageable steps. Gradually increasing the duration and complexity of somatic practices allows for a natural and sustainable progression over time. Therefore, it is important to let your somatic practice start off small and comfortable before naturally unfolding into a fully established routine.
- **Consistency over intensity**: It's better to work with somatic practices for five minutes every day than it is to work with them for five hours in one day one time a month. Therefore, try to prioritize the consistency of your practice over the intensity of it.
- **Flexibility**: Be sure that you allow yourself a degree of flexibility when it comes to the timing and extent of your practice. Every day is going to be different, which means you might have to alter your plans. Moreover, allow yourself to be flexible enough to adapt your practices to fit alongside new goals.
- **Explore diverse practices**: Don't be afraid to try something new every once in a while to spice up your practice and make sure that you're using the best methods for your goals.

Building Resilience in the Face of Setbacks

As you work to heal, it is important to recognize that setbacks are a natural part of the journey. Acknowledging setbacks as a natural part of this transformative process is crucial. Therefore, understanding how you can build resilience in the face of setbacks is crucial. Rather than perceiving setbacks as roadblocks, framing them as temporary detours or opportunities for redirection can facilitate a more constructive mindset. In other words, viewing setbacks through a lens of growth fosters resilience. You can work to be more resilient by engaging with:

- **Mindful self-reflection**: Engaging in mindful self-reflection during particularly stressful times or times of resistance can be a powerful way to work through blocks. This introspective process promotes a deeper understanding of triggers and patterns as well, highlighting potential explanations for why you're frustrated, impatient, or facing a blockage.
- **Seeking support and connection**: Seeking support and connection from others who make use of somatic therapy practices, both in real life and through online forums, can be uplifting when it comes to struggles. Beyond that, a support network of those in similar circumstances can even help offer advice to overcome those struggles.
- **Setting realistic expectations**: Resilience is also built by setting realistic expectations. Setting hard to reach goals might seem motivating, but they can actually serve to let you down and cause bigger challenges. Having realistic expectations for your somatic therapy practice will be more rewarding in the end.

Beyond that, some strategies that will help you further bounce back from challenges include:

- **Incremental progress**: View recovery as a series of sprints rather than a marathon race. When you do this, breaking your big goals down into smaller ones, you gain consistent progress and reduce setbacks and lack of motivation.
- **Learn from setbacks**: Each setback holds valuable lessons. Adopting a mindset that seeks to understand and learn from setbacks transforms them into opportunities for personal and somatic growth.
- **Be flexible**: Being open to adjusting somatic practices or therapeutic approaches in response to setbacks allows for a flexible and adaptive healing journey. Flexibility ensures that you can explore what truly resonates with you.

Alongside that, it is important to cultivate a positive mindset for your journey—which will enhance resilience and your ability to overcome struggles as a result. For example, it is a good idea to develop a sense of optimism for your journey and for the process of healing. Celebrate victories to cultivate a positive mindset that empowers you to appreciate your progress. You should make sure that your perspective is always—or as much as possible—geared toward the positive aspects of healing. Rather than focusing on how far you have left to go, for instance, focus on how far you've come.

Affirmations can also help counteract the negative thought patterns that you experience during a setback or block. Affirmations like "I am right where I need to be" can be comforting and reinforce your progress. Moreover, positive self-talk and compassion can steer you away from being angry about a lack of progress or down about the journey.

Furthermore, developing a growth mindset can be powerful when it comes to revoking doubtful mindsets. A growth mindset says that you have the power to learn, grow, and change in any way necessary or desired. It means that you don't have to let success happen to you—you can pursue it, which inherently involves setbacks that teach you lessons and help you grow.

Planning for Continued Growth and Healing

The last major concept we have to explore is how you can plan for the future of continued growth and healing when it comes to your somatic journey.

Setting Realistic Goals for the Future

Somatic therapy, both from the beginning and when it comes to paving a positive future, hinges on setting achievable and realistic goals. By celebrating small milestones as essential markers of progress, you can foster a sustainable and rewarding path to ongoing somatic growth. Beyond that, goals can keep you motivated and help you understand where your efforts should be placed, which is known to improve goal-related success.

In order to set goals for your ongoing somatic therapy journey, it is important to identify your personal priorities. Try answering "what matters the most to you when it comes to your somatic journey?" in just one sentence, or even one word. This can help you understand what priorities you want to focus on. Understanding what aspects of growth are most important allows for targeted and meaningful goal-setting.

Then, you should break bigger goals down into smaller ones. Take the biggest goal that you have and write down what goals you need to meet along the way that stack up to that bigger goal. This helps you work on smaller goals that get you to your bigger goal, rather than overwhelming you by looking at such a big goal out of the gate. Plus, with each bite-sized goal you accomplish, you'll get closer and closer to success while boosting your confidence as well.

And while it is good to shoot for the stars when it comes to your success, you also have to be able to understand and consider your personal limitations. No one is perfect, and that includes you and your recovery process. With that being said, your personal pace of growth is going to be unique. You can set a goal to meet within a month, but you might find that it takes you closer to three or four months to achieve it. That's fine! It doesn't mean that you or your goal have failed, just that you need to be flexible.

When it comes to realistic goals, flexibility is key. Obviously, this is your first time working with somatic therapy in this way, so even if you give yourself leeway with your initial goals, you'll still need to be flexible. This means that you should know what your plans are for busy days, days where you can't practice at all, unexpected breaks and lack of motivation, and more. These contingency plans and the ability to go with the flow is invaluable to a strong, sustained practice.

Additionally, part of setting realistic goals for the journey is recognizing that somatic therapy is a lifelong process. Even if you "heal" from your trauma in a complete way, in order to maintain that healing and wellness, you have to continue your practice. Think of is this way—someone who takes antidepressants can't stop their medication once they feel better; it is because of the medication that they feel better in the first place.

This means that somatic therapy should be a regular part of your life even when you feel like it is done the job. Using the simple and short methods for awareness, release, and integration can make somatic therapy easy, even if you live a busy life. Making time for your well-being is crucial regardless, and somatic therapy is especially flexible.

Exploring Advanced Somatic Practices

As you walk along the path of your somatic therapy journey, you may find yourself at a point where you need more advanced tactics to deepen the practice. That's no problem. There are advanced somatic therapy tactics that go beyond foundational techniques, delving into more intricate and nuanced approaches to engage the mind-body connection. These practices often involve a deeper exploration of sensations, emotions, and the integration of diverse modalities.

At the same time, you do need to be well-versed in the more fundamental practices mentioned thus far. It may seem like jumping right into advanced practices will catapult you toward healing, but the reality is that that's not the case. Starting ahead of your readiness level can be discouraging when you don't make the progress you expect, which is why starting with more foundational practices before venturing into more advanced terrain is important.

When you feel ready to work with advanced practices, you should make sure that that exploration is progressive. Explore one technique at a time, allowing for a gradual integration that aligns with your individual comfort levels and pacing. If you find yourself to be at the precipice of an advanced level, this is a great time to tap into the personal experiences of others and the guidance of professionals. Their expertise can provide tailored recommendations and ensure a safe and supportive exploration of more intricate practices.

Somatic therapy is also ever-evolving. This means that the practices you pick up now will be foundational, but new and advanced tactics will be explored, expanded, and even created all of the time. Embrace somatic therapy as a constant flux of learning and adaptation so that you can remain open to new insights and developments. The benefit of doing so is that your practice will be both more rewarding and more personal! By considering advanced options for somatic therapy, you can empower yourself to explore your inner world more, as well as uncover more modalities and options.

Integration Into Lifestyle and Well-Being

To attain a holistic sense of well-being, your somatic practices have to be integrated into various aspects of your lifestyle. I cannot stress enough how this ongoing commitment and effort is crucial to your journey and success.

The mind-body connection is just one fundamental aspect of well-being that you have to keep in mind throughout every step of the process. Understanding this mind-body connection reinforces the importance of integrating somatic practices into everyday experiences. Beyond that, recognizing that mental and physical health are intertwined fosters a holistic approach to overall well-being.

When you use somatic practices, you have to recognize that they serve as a foundational component of well-being, underscoring their role in promoting balance, resilience, and emotional regulation. This foundation serves as a cornerstone for navigating life's challenges with greater ease and self-awareness. To recount, some of the methods you can use to ensure this daily interaction and integration include

- **Mindful work breaks**: Incorporate short somatic practices during work breaks, such as mindful breathing or gentle stretching, to refresh the mind and release tension.
- **Body awareness at the desk**: Practice body awareness while working by periodically checking in with posture, releasing tension in the shoulders, and taking mindful pauses to prevent stress buildup.

- **Embodied communication**: Infuse somatic awareness into communication by paying attention to body language, gestures, and subtle cues. This fosters more authentic and connected interactions.

Keeping your practices consistent is probably the single most important thing you can do on your journey. Whether you work with five minutes of somatic exercises a day or engage with somatic therapy periodically throughout the day, this consistency paves the way to a lifelong journey patterned with growth, healing, and wellness.

Company makes the road less lonely. Remember that you also always have the option of going out to meet others who prioritize their somatic well-being just like you do. This can be through classes, group therapy opportunities, online forums and groups, and even by asking friends and family to engage with somatic practices alongside you. Who knows, you may just start a chain reaction of somatic wellness!

Our journey together is closing, but your journey with somatic therapy is just getting started! It's time to pave the road to a better and brighter future for yourself thanks to somatic therapy interventions.

CONCLUSION

Much like healing isn't a universal journey, trauma is complicated and tailored to the individual. Even if two people experience a car crash or assault, those two people experience such circumstances very differently. It might seem like this means everyone needs drastically different therapeutic methods, but one method stands out as a beacon of hope with the ability to be endlessly personalized: somatic therapy.

Somatic therapy encourages the mind-body connection in a way that other methods of therapy don't. It takes a look at how the trauma, experiences, and emotions you have can manifest through the body in a physical way, also highlighting how we can release such things.

In a world where therapeutic methods, even the best among the best, leave trauma survivors in pain, confused, and reaching for alternative options, somatic therapy is powerful. And now, you have everything it takes to embrace self-guided somatic therapy safely and from the comfort of your own home. Now, you know

- what somatic therapy is and the benefits it can provide you regarding your recovery.

- the elusive connection between trauma and the body—even if your trauma wasn't physical—and how this can supercharge your healing
- assessing, releasing, and integrating: the powerful 3-step method for self-guided somatic therapy
- how to integrate your personal efforts alongside other forms of therapy.

And much more. Beyond that, you've gained the unparalleled power to take control of your recovery. It's a powerful thing that no one can take away from you.

If you've appreciated this resource, please consider leaving a review; that way, others seeking the same recovery and relief options can find this resource. If you're interested in other self-guided therapeutic methods, I have another book on eye movement desensitization reprocessing (EMDR) therapy that you might want to consider as well.

Overall, the journey of somatic therapy can be empowering, enlightening, and freeing. Thank you for coming along with me on this journey. Now, it's time for you to put the skills you've harnessed to use and pave a road to a more freeing, welcoming future that favors your comfort. You've got this!

THANK YOU

First and foremost, I want to express my heartfelt gratitude for choosing my book. In a world brimming with options, you took a chance on this one, and I couldn't be more thankful for your trust and commitment to exploring its pages.

As you reach the end of this journey, I have a small favor to ask. Would you consider sharing your thoughts by posting a review on the platform where you acquired the book? Your review isn't just a few words; it's an invaluable source of support for independent authors like myself.

Your feedback serves as a guiding light, allowing me to continue crafting books that resonate with your needs and aspirations. Hearing from you means the world to me, and it fuels my passion for writing.

Once again, thank you for your time, trust, and support. Your review will make a significant difference in our literary voyage together

>> Leave a review on Amazon US <<

>> Leave a review on Amazon UK <<

BONUS CONTENT

As a token of my appreciation for your purchase, I'm delighted to offer you the Meditation for Beginners Mini Book for FREE.

To access this bonus instantly, simply visit:

bit.ly/free_bonus_content

REFERENCES

Ackerman, C. (2017, January 18). *22 Mindfulness Exercises, Techniques & Activities For Adults (+ PDF's)*. PositivePsychology.com. https://positivepsychology.com/mindfulness-exercises-techniques-activities/

ACRM. (2020, March 31). *Rehabilitation Research: Somatic Exercise and Trauma Recovery*. ACRM. https://acrm.org/rehabilitation-medicine/somatic-exercises-and-trauma-recovery/

An Easy 6-Step Somatic Exercise to Process Triggers — Integrative Psychotherapy Mental Health Blog. (n.d.). Integrative Psychotherapy & Trauma Treatment. https://integrativepsych.co/new-blog/somatic-therapy-five-towns

Aybar, S. (2021, July 21). *4 At-Home Somatic Therapy Exercises for Trauma Recovery*. Psych Central. https://psychcentral.com/lib/somatic-therapy-exercises-for-trauma

Bachert, A. (2023, August 2). *Somatic Exercises to Improve Your Mental Health*. Charlie Health. https://www.charliehealth.com/post/somatic-exercises-for-mental-health

Bakal, D., Coll, P., & Schaefer, J. (2008). Somatic awareness in the clinical care of patients with body distress symptoms. *BioPsychoSocial Medicine, 2*(1). https://doi.org/10.1186/1751-0759-2-6

Begley, M. (2022, March 14). *What is Somatic Awareness? What is Somatic Therapy?* Edelson & Associates. https://edelsonandassociates.info/2022/03/14/what-is-somatic-awareness-what-is-somatic-therapy/

Blanchfield, T. (2023, November 20). *What to Know About Somatic Experiencing Therapy*. Verywell Mind. Retrieved December 31, 2023, from https://www.verywellmind.com/what-is-somatic-experiencing-5204186#:~:text=Created%20by%20Peter%20Levine%2C%20PhD

Christy. (2021, January 2). *Grounding and Centering*. Wayward Inspiration. https://waywardinspiration.com/grounding-and-centering/

Elliott, P. (2016, July 5). *8 Self Help Tips from Somatic Experiencing Trauma Therapy*. Courage Counseling, PLLC. https://courage-counseling.com/somatic-experiencing-self-help-tips/

Hippocrates. (n.d.). *Hippocrates: 'Healing is a matter of time, but it is sometimes also a matter of opportunity'.* The Socratic Method. https://www.socratic-method.com/quote-meanings/hippocrates-healing-is-a-matter-of-time-but-it-is-sometimes-also-a-matter-of-opportunity

How Common Is PTSD in Adults? (n.d.). PTSD: National Center for PTSD. https://www.ptsd.va.gov/understand/common/common_adults.asp

How Trauma is Stored in the Body | D'Amore Mental Health. (2022, November 21). Damorementalhealth.com. https://damorementalhealth.com/resources/how-trauma-is-stored-in-the-body/

Kelloway, R. (2023, February 3). *5 Somatic Experiencing Techniques That Anyone Can Use to Stay Grounded.* Life Care Wellness. https://life-care-wellness.com/5-somatic-experiencing-techniques-that-anyone-can-use-to-stay-grounded/

Kirstein, M. (2023, October 7). *12 Effective Somatic Therapy Exercises for Holistic Healing.* Www.monakirstein.com. https://www.monakirstein.com/somatic-therapy-exercises/

Krouse, L. (2023, August 11). *A Comprehensive Guide to Somatic Therapy.* EverydayHealth.com. https://www.everydayhealth.com/emotional-health/somatic-therapy/

Laoutaris, N. (2023, December 15). *Somatic therapy exercises and techniques.* Www.firstsession.com. https://www.firstsession.com/resources/somatic-therapy-exercises-techniques

Lebow, H. (2022, September 14). *How Does Your Body Remember Trauma? Plus 5 Ways to Heal.* Psych Central. https://psychcentral.com/health/how-your-body-remembers-trauma

Martensson, Jonatan. (n.d.). *Quotes.* Goodreads. https://www.goodreads.com/quotes/670136-feelings-are-much-like-waves-we-can-t-stop-them-from

McDonald, Jorie. (2023). *36 Healing Quotes For Inspiration And Encouragement.* https://www.southernliving.com/culture/healing-quotes

Mindfulness exercises. (2020, September 15). Mayo Clinic. https://www.mayoclinic.org/healthy-lifestyle/consumer-health/in-depth/mindfulness-exercises/art-20046356

Moniuszko, S. M. (2022, January 20). *Trauma isn't just psychological. It can impact your body too.* USA TODAY. https://www.usatoday.com/story/life/health-wellness/2022/01/20/trauma-physical-impact-body-how-to-release/6562449001/

Naomi Remen, Rachel. (n.d.). *Rachel Naomi Remen Quotes.* Goodreads. https://www.goodreads.com/quotes/491458-healing-may-not-be-so-much-about-getting-better-as

Nunez, K. (2023, April 27). *7 Ways to Be More Mindful Without Meditating.* SELF. https://www.self.com/story/best-mindfulness-exercises

Pedersen, T. (2021, August 18). *Somatic Therapy: How It Works, Uses, Types, and Techniques.* Psych Central. https://psychcentral.com/blog/how-somatic-therapy-can-help-patients-suffering-from-psychological-trauma

Raypole, C. (2019, May 24). *30 grounding techniques to quiet distressing thoughts.* Healthline. https://www.healthline.com/health/grounding-techniques

Rodenhauser, A. (n.d.). Self-administered EMDR without a therapist is very useful for a lot of things! *www.lesswrong.com.* Retrieved January 12, 2024, from https://www.lesswrong.com/posts/peQpvaaSTjmkxDudB/self-administered-emdr-without-a-therapist-is-very-useful

Salamon, M. (2023, July 7). *What is somatic therapy?* Harvard Health. https://www.health.harvard.edu/blog/what-is-somatic-therapy-202307072951

Self Administered EMDR: How to do EMDR yourself. Can you do it DIY? (2023, July 17). https://turboemdr.com/self-administered-emdr-how-to-yourself-can-you/

Somatic Self Care. (n.d.). www.hopkinsmedicine.org. https://www.hopkinsmedicine.org/office-of-well-being/connection-support/somatic-self-care

10 mindfulness exercises to include in your daily routine. (2023, September 1). Calm Blog. https://www.calm.com/blog/mindfulness-exercises

van der Kolk, Bessel. (2014). *The Body Keeps the Score.*

Made in the USA
Las Vegas, NV
23 September 2024